DAD ON PURPOSE

THE BUSY DAD'S PLAYBOOK FOR LOVING BETTER, DOING MORE AND BREATHING EASIER

TIM DUNN

-A Dadathlon Series Book-

Copyright © 2021 by Tim Dunn

Dad On Purpose: The Busy Dad's Playbook for Loving Better, Doing More and Breathing Easier

All rights reserved. No part of this publication may be reproduced, distributed or transmitted in any form or by any means, including photocopying, recording, or other electronic or mechanical methods, without the prior written permission of the publisher, except in the case of brief quotations embodied in critical reviews and certain other noncommercial uses permitted by copyright law.

Although the author and publisher have made every effort to ensure that the information in this book was correct at press time, the author and publisher do not assume and hereby disclaim any liability to any party for any loss, damage, or disruption caused by errors or omissions, whether such errors or omissions result from negligence, accident, or any other cause.

Adherence to all applicable laws and regulations, including international, federal, state and local governing professional licensing, business practices, advertising, and all other aspects of doing business in the US, Canada or any other jurisdiction is the sole responsibility of the reader and consumer.

Neither the author nor the publisher assumes any responsibility or liability whatsoever on behalf of the consumer or reader of this material. Any perceived slight of any individual or organization is purely unintentional.

The resources in this book are provided for informational purposes only and should not be used to replace the specialized training and professional judgment of a health care or mental health care professional.

Neither the author nor the publisher can be held responsible for the use of the information provided within this book. Please always consult a trained professional before making any decision regarding treatment of yourself or others.

ISBN: 978-1-7379461-0-6

DOWNLOAD THE AUDIOBOOK FREE!

READ THIS FIRST

As a thank you for downloading my book, I would like to give you the audiobook version **100% FREE**

TO DOWNLOAD GO TO:
http://www.DadAthlon.com/FreeAudio

PLUS get a free bonus list of essential movies to watch with your kids.

Never waste another half hour trying to find the perfect movie to watch!

DEDICATION

For my dad—thankful for your example.

For Erin—thankful for your love, support, and inspiration.

For my kids—thankful for every fiber of your being, more than you will ever know.

Your smiles and challenges inspire me daily to be a better dad and a better man.

CONTENTS

1. How to Use This Book 1

PART 1 — LOVING BETTER - CONNECTING WITH… 13

2. Connecting With Daughters 17
3. Connecting With Sons 35
4. Connecting With Mom 47

PART 2 — DOING MORE - PROVIDING 63

5. Execution 65
6. Dollars - Defense 85
7. Dollars - Offense 113

PART 3 — BREATHING EASIER - LIVING 135

8. Health 139
9. Joy 155
10. Wisdom 171

PART 4 — NOW WHAT? 181

11. Game Time 183

APPENDIX A – Dad Hacks and Bonuses 187
APPENDIX B – Dos and Don'ts 199
APPENDIX C – Useful Links 207
APPENDIX D – Other Great Books 213

Acknowledgments 215
About the Author 217

CHAPTER 1

HOW TO USE THIS BOOK

"Being a great father is like shaving. No matter how good you shaved today, you have to do it again tomorrow."

– Reed Markham

I don't have many crystal-clear memories of my average childhood day. I recall big events and vacations and fun times with my friends, but the details of most days fade into a general familiar mist of being a kid.

However, there's one exception: I vividly remember one otherwise sleepy car ride with absolute clarity. Not because there was an accident or argument or some crazy spectacle we drove past. I was simply on the way to my little league baseball game.

It was 1987. I was twelve years old, and my dad was taking me to the game after a long day of school. Driving in the car with my dad, we naturally had the radio on—this was long before iPhones or any phones that weren't connected to a wall. Dad was always pretty even-keeled; he certainly was not a man with strongly-voiced opinions about music on the radio. His was a steady, patient, and quiet strength supporting our family. We rarely observed intense or immediate action unless someone was in danger.

But on this day, as we rumbled along Griswold Street in my hometown of Wethersfield, Connecticut, a familiar song came on. The moment it began, he moved immediately to change the station. I can still see his arm shooting over to the radio buttons like a laser to hit *any* other button. I was temporarily stunned by this uncharacteristically abrupt move.

"You okay, Dad?"

"I just don't like that song."

I might have asked, "Why don't you like it?" at that unusual moment. But I didn't. At that time, I was a mindless, self-absorbed boy on his way to a baseball game, which was as far as my curiosity at that moment would take me. So I shrugged my shoulders and went back to what I was doing, which was looking out the window blankly.

Only later that night did I process what happened. What the song was. How deeply baked into his bones was my dad's aversion to that song, which begins, "My child arrived just the other day. He came to the world in the usual way…"

Harry Chapin's classic "Cat's in the Cradle" pulls at heartstrings young and old. It recounts a young father whose busy life crowds out the quality time his son craves. The son repeatedly expresses how much he idolizes his father with "I'm gonna be like you, Dad. You know I'm gonna be like you."

The boy eventually grows into a young father himself, busy with a new job and sick kids. His father, now retired with time and perspective, calls his son to see if they can get together. The boy responds with, "I'd love to, Dad, if I can find the time. You see, my new job's a hassle, and the kids have the flu, but it's been sure nice talking to you, Dad. It's been sure nice talking to you."

The pensive, regretful, and now lonely father then observes, "And as I hung up the phone, it occurred to me, he'd grown up just like me. My boy was just like me."

This was the song my dad had zero tolerance for. Every time I hear it now, I absorb every word. Today, upon reflection, I understand how much my dad loved his family and how he constructed his own life to ensure he was always there for us.

Early in his career, he was a lawyer and found a job at a prestigious law firm with a promising future. But as with many law firms, such promise comes at the cost of long and unpredictable hours. As a father of four boys, his priority was to balance providing with being there for my mom and us. He left the firm and took a job working for a government agency with stable hours. This freed him up to provide for us and be present at games and events and in the backyard.

I don't recall any specific instances of Dad practicing grounders in the backyard with my brothers and me or working on pop-ups with a racquetball. But that is because it happened so regularly; it was woven into the fabric of our lives in the same way I remember sitting around the table for dinners, but not any single meal.

Similarly, I'm sure there were a few high school cross country meets he couldn't attend. But I cannot recall competing in a single one without seeing my dad there. And let me assure you, there is no spectator sport in the world more boring than sixty gangly boys running into the woods, then emerging fifteen minutes later!

During my entire childhood, I took all that for granted. He was just there. Like dads are. Duh!

Only now, with four children of my own, do I see much more clearly how difficult and *deliberate* his efforts were. Being a great dad is no accident; you can only achieve that when you decide to dad *on purpose*. Only now do I see clearly that the word "dad" is as much a verb as it is a noun. It requires planning, effort, grit, and above all, balance.

Finding balance is challenging, and doing it right is not guaranteed. As a dad, you are busy as hell, moving in a hundred directions at once. No one in your house really gets it. And no one shuts off the damn lights!

It is your job to balance…

> the quality time needed to connect with each person in the house…
>
> with the necessary logistics of providing for the family…
>
> while concurrently living a fulfilled life of joy and wisdom.

Sound familiar?

Connecting, providing, and living well require very different skills, but each is critical to being a successful father. In a triathlon, a great swimmer may not be a good runner because each skill uses a different muscle group. Only when someone adequately balances them all can he become a successful triathlete.

This book offers simple strategies and "workouts" to help busy dads build balanced strength across the three muscle groups of the dad-triathlon—the DadAthlon: Connecting, Providing, and Living.

In the same way that a workout book breaks down chapters into legs, arms, back, and abs, this book breaks down the various muscle groups of dad-ness. Each chapter discusses the importance of the muscle group as well as its application in the real world. Some have specific workouts you might consider trying, and others share resources you may find useful. Many ideas are common sense, others you may not have considered. All are simple, effective, and intended to help you build the dad muscle group you decide to work on.

Connecting

Chapters two through four focus on the softer skills of being a dad, specifically ways to connect with the people who matter most. Our daughters, our sons, and our wife (or kids' mom) each have unique needs. It is common for a dad to spend so much time providing that he forgets to build and maintain real connections with the exact people he is providing for. We all love our families but sometimes struggle with exactly how to love them. These chapters will help us *love better.*

Providing

Chapters five through seven focus on planning and paying for the necessary things we provide for our families. Chapter five focuses on execution with insights into setting and achieving goals. The following two chapters concentrate on financial strategies. Chapter six explores defense, where we protect money going out the door. Chapter seven pivots to offense, which shares tools and ideas on ways to bring more money in the door. There are only so many hours in a day to get things done. These chapters will help us *do more*.

Living

Finally, we each need to live a fulfilling life that is both worthy of itself and an example to our children. This section discusses strategies for maximizing our physical and mental health, creating and capturing joy, and seeking and sharing wisdom. In so doing, these chapters allow us to *breathe easier*.

Along the way, we'll share many additional concrete resources. These fall into two categories:

> Dad-hacks—simple and effective tricks or tools.

> Bonus —useful extra resources or observations, including online quizzes or tools, often customized to your specific needs.

Each chapter ends with a summary and a list of dos and don'ts related to the action steps discussed.

What This Book is NOT

Before we dig in further, I want to take a brief moment to clarify what this book is NOT.

It's NOT Holier-than-thou

I am not writing this book because I am super-dad with all the answers, eager to dad-shame other men to feel better about myself. Let's get this out of the way at the outset—while I want to be an awesome dad, my past efforts have often fallen far short.

I can assure you, I approach this fully aware of my many lapses. To prove it, allow me to share the following abridged list of some of my lowest dad moments:

- I once left for Thanksgiving dinner and forgot one of my kids.
- I've cursed both at and in front of my kids. Often.
- I didn't start saving for college as early as I should have.
- I sometimes let the goddamn devices win.
- I have dealt with the stress of a long day/week by drinking too much.
- I have hidden in the basement/bedroom/bathroom because I am too damn tired to do the right dad thing.
- I have played dumb on difficult issues and let mom do the heavy lifting.

I don't share those with you because I want to, and certainly not because I am proud of them. I share them so you know I am approaching this book as someone who has failed early and often in my role as a dad. I'm a guy who has learned from his mistakes, who wants better for himself and his kids, and who may slip again but will get back up with a plan. Maybe that sounds like you too.

I share this so you know I am not some guru on a mountain with secret dad-knowledge from the Jedi texts. Rather I am a fellow seeker of simple strategies that work in the messy chaos of our lives today.

This book is simply a catalog of some great strategies I've found along the way to help us all be better, saner, happier dads.

It's NOT Exhaustive

Much more has been and will continue to be written on all of the topics in each chapter of this book. This book's goal is neither to invent new strategies nor to explore every possible nuance under the sun that might impact success in these areas.

Instead, this book will provide proven, easy, actionable ideas to make progress in the areas of dad-ness you most want to improve. It is neither a guidebook to a sweeping lifestyle change, nor a clickbait list of Will Smith's celebrity life hacks for dads—you won't believe #8!

Think of this book as living in the space between a diet recipe book and an 8-minute-abs coach. There are plenty of options to pick from to get healthy, and your coach can help you figure out where to start. Find a few recipes or workouts that work for you and start working them into your life one at a time.

It's NOT the End

This book is only the first step of building a community of dads sharing valuable ideas, tools, and support. While you'll find many useful ideas on these pages, I encourage you to build on this foundation through interactive online resources. Check us out at www.DadAthlon.com and on Twitter @DadAthlon and Facebook's DadAthlon page. Building an active community ensures we stay relevant to the concerns of today's dads with real-time resources and value. Together, we will build ourselves into world-class DadAthletes.

Why This Book

Take a moment and picture yourself as an eighty-year-old man. Your kids are grown and on their own, and most of the heavy-lifting of your fatherhood is now in your past. How often do you see your kids and grandkids? Are they happy? Are they successful? Are they resentful or thankless? As you reflect on their future lives, how much of their happiness and success is because of you? Or despite you? When future-you calls them on the phone to get together, have they "grown up just like you?"

Does the answer to that last question make you happy or nervous?

What aspects of today's version of you would you most love your kids to inherit? Which ones terrify you?

Guess what, today's you will have a direct impact on the story that eighty-year-old man will tell. Glimpsing the present from a fictitious future, you are both George Bailey and Ebenezer Scrooge. You can re-write that version of your life into the dad-story you look back upon with satisfaction, fulfillment, and warmth.

What events will your re-written story contain?

That's where this book comes in. The goal of this book is not to develop or share groundbreaking research on every nuance of fatherhood and relationships. Rather my goals are simple:

> Identify which aspects of your fatherhood *you* believe need strengthening.

> Provide easy, actionable ideas for you to build those muscles.

This book will equip you with strategies, events, and ideas you need to populate your re-written story.

How to Use This Book

In a triathlon, some guys are natural runners but can't swim. Some are great swimmers but can't ride a bike well. This book will help you find areas that need work and offer simple proven workouts to build that skill. Then when you've mastered that, find the next area for growth until you are the world-class DadAthlete you see in your mind's eye.

The first step is to get clarity on your highest priority. In the above triathlon scenario, if you used to run years ago but have never swum before, spending the first few weeks focusing on swimming makes sense. Work on the strokes and the mechanics of swimming first to build that skill. It is the area where you have the most to gain; it's where you'll have the highest leverage.

As you look at the list of chapters/skills, there are likely a few you're nailing every day and feel great about. But you'll certainly find others you wish weren't on the list—chapters you may be nervous to read because they act as a mirror to known weaknesses. Others may include a task you know is essential but difficult. Start there. Keep it simple. Once you have that squared away, add the next highest leverage skill.

> Dad Hack: Take the Quiz. What kind of dad are you? To help you prioritize which areas you may want to begin with, visit www.DadAthlon.com/DadQuiz. You will find a simple set of questions to provide clarity and direction on where to begin. This guidance provides insight into which muscle groups will benefit most from focused attention.

IMPORTANT: You may be tempted to implement a handful of these strategies all on day one. Don't! In my experience, when you focus on everything, you focus on nothing. Start small with something very simple until you've mastered it. Then add the next thing. When you build a skyscraper, you don't assemble all the floors at once; you build it one floor at a time from the ground up. Very few of these steps take long to put in place, so be patient. The best plan is the one that gets done, and it is easier to do one thing than many. So start with one until it is second nature. Then add another one.

Summary

You are busy as hell trying to do it all. Just like an elite triathlete builds strength across different muscle groups, a truly awesome dad develops specific skills in the three muscle groups of connecting with his family, providing for his household, and living his life well.

This book is not an exhaustive guide on All-Things-Dad. It is a series of valuable tools for busy dads to improve the areas that need the most attention, one workout at a time.

Reviewing your decisions today from the perspective of your future children will provide clarity and motivation as you begin the training to become a world-class DadAthlete.

Do

- ➢ Read the whole book.
- ➢ Take the assessment at www.DadAthlon.com/DadQuiz.
- ➢ Pick *one* area to focus on first.
- ➢ Reread the chapter on your primary area of focus and implement your first strategy until it's mastered.

> If you still need to build strength, pick a new strategy in the same chapter, focusing on one at a time until you feel good about your progress.

Then...

> Move on to your next highest area of focus.
> Repeat.
> Join the Facebook Group
> Follow us on Twitter @DadAthlon

Don't

> Implement multiple strategies at the same time
> Get discouraged after a bad day/week/month

> **FYI**: I am in a male/female relationship. As a result, this book uses language and pronouns that are consistent with my experience. In so doing, I am not saying other types of relationships are undesirable or unhealthy—only that they are not my experience. The goal of this book is to share what I've learned as a father—things I've tried and failed, where I've researched and found success, and things we can improve together as we all learn. While I'm hopeful fathers in all types of relationships may find value in these pages, my silence on other types of relationships is only in recognition of my limitations on such matters—others far better equipped than I can explore the unique challenges such dads face.

PART 1
LOVING BETTER – CONNECTING WITH...

> The price of anything is the amount of life you exchange for it.
>
> – Henry David Thoreau

I hate the Cheesecake Factory. Don't get me wrong, their cheesecake is fantastic, and I'm as pro-cheesecake as the next guy. The food, portions, and service are likewise all fine. My problem with them isn't the food or the service—it's the damn menu! You might as well walk in there and get a menu on a Post-It note that simply reads "Any food that exists in the world."

When the menu of options is so large and broad, it can be hard to know where to begin. You might even fall into paralysis by analysis—spending so much time wondering which option is perfect that you never actually pick anything.

In our house, this sometimes manifests on a Friday night when we are too tired to cook, so we decide it might be nice to go out for dinner. This has led to conversations like the abbreviated one below:

"Where do you want to go for dinner tonight?"

"I don't know. Where do *you* want to go for dinner?"

"I'm up for anything. Just happy to grab a nice meal after a long week. What's the first place that pops into your head?"

"I don't have any strong preferences. I guess we went to seafood last time, so maybe something different?"

"Any other types of restaurants you *don't* want?"

"I don't know."

"Me neither. My brain is fried. Plus, it's probably too late to get a table anyplace soon—let's just have cereal and leftovers on the couch."

Have you ever had a conversation like that? By the end of a long week, if we decide to go out for dinner, our brains are so tapped they don't want to do any more heavy lifting. Even for something fun. Narrowing a universe of options down to one is both intimidating and taxing.

A small number of options, however, creates clarity. Compare the above conversation with this one.

"Where do you want to go for dinner tonight—pizza or Chinese?"

"We had Chinese last time, so let's grab pizza. I'll get the kids."

Okay, I get it. That's not necessarily how that conversation always goes. But this approach creates clarity and focused action much better than the first one did. In our house, every time we begin our Friday dinner conversation this way, our couch is lonely.

What does this have to do with being a dad and connecting with our loved ones?

I initially wanted to begin this book with the section on providing. It is so important and probably where most men want to dive in first. If you're reading this now, you understand that fatherhood is about more than only providing resources and opportunities. We also need to *father* our children, to understand and connect with them. They are the deepest *why* behind all our providing. As the opening quote of this section suggests, life is a series of trade-offs. As dads, we need to balance providing with connecting. These awesome and fragile people are desperate for our attention, guidance, and love.

Sometimes the prospect of connecting with our family *too* much might terrify us. Conversations may get real, or we're not sure what to say or do.

If you're like me, you may often want to be "doing something" with the kids, but what? What is the perfect activity, movie to watch, or game to play? It's like trying to figure out dinner on Friday. In the absence of clear, crisp options, it's easy to hem and haw and not come up with anything worthwhile until we end up all having cereal. Meanwhile, the kids are mindlessly Snapchatting and TikToking, and we fall asleep in the middle of episode 6 of Game of Thrones. Or dang—maybe it was episode 5?

Tired at the end of a long day, we mentally run through the vague, formless cloud of all human activities the kids might enjoy. The goal of the following chapters is to create clear options for time with our kids by asking, "Pizza or Chinese?"

These are not intended to be comprehensive lists but a starting menu of options to consider as well as a mechanism to prime your pump. In the second conversation above, you may not actually end up eating pizza *or* Chinese. But the act of expressing those two distinct options clearly gets our brain thinking in concrete terms rather than abstract.

The reply might be: "I don't want pizza or Chinese, but that new Mexican place just opened across from the pizza place. Let's do that." Even then, you end up making a decision that is both better and sooner than the first conversation.

The following two chapters will discuss some of the unique differences between boys and girls and will provide clear menu options. Our goal is to focus on easy and actionable options targeted for you and your son or daughter. Rather than sections for appetizers, entrees, and desserts, our menus will be divided into do, read, watch, play, write and model. The final chapter of the section shifts our focus to the unique ways we can better support, partner with, and appreciate our kids' mom.

CHAPTER 2

CONNECTING WITH DAUGHTERS

Fathers be good to your daughters. Daughters will love like you do…You are the god and the weight of her world.

– John Mayer

When my wife and I were first married, we lived in separate states for a few years. While she was in graduate school in Syracuse, New York, I worked in Hartford, Connecticut, about four hours away. I drove back and forth each weekend, which wasn't ideal, but we were still five years away from having our first kid. We focused on work during the week and each other during the weekend. We also learned a valuable lesson on how to compartmentalize our time.

I was a huge audiobook nerd then—and now! Back then, I had to get books on CD out of the library. On one trip, my external CD player broke, so I had to listen to the radio. As I was driving along the New York Thruway one Friday evening in 1998 just west of Albany, a song came on the radio I had never heard before. It began,

"There's two things I know for sure: She was sent here from heaven and she's daddy's little girl…."

Before continuing, I should pause for two quick observations:

1) While I'm certainly not captain tough-guy, I am also not super emotional. The last time I could recall crying was at my grandfather's funeral when I was ten.
2) In 1998, I did not yet have *any* children, much less an adorable little girl.

The song continues with the father listening to his little girl praying by her bed, asking him to walk beside her pony, and apologizing that the cake she made for him looks funny. And through it all, the dad thanks God for having done something right to deserve *"a hug every morning and butterfly kisses at night."*

So at this point, my throat tightens a bit. But it's cool. It's just a song—and a nice one—but let's see where it goes…

She grows into a teenager in the next verse, which continues, *"One part woman, the other part girl. To perfume and makeup from ribbons and curls… 'you know how much I love you daddy, but if you don't mind, I'm only gonna kiss you on the cheek this time…'"*

Ahem. There are few moments more surreal than being alone in your car and fake-clearing your throat to shake off the welling emotions in a vain attempt to reassert your manhood in front of …yourself!

And then…

"She'll change her name today. She'll make a promise and I'll give her away. Standing in the bride-room just staring at her. She asked me what I'm thinking and I said I'm not sure—I just feel like I'm losing my baby girl."

God! Dang! Blowing air slowly out of puffed cheeks, happy to see an upcoming rest stop, I put my blinker on and make my way to the right lane to pull off, when I hear the following:

"*She leaned over, Gave me butterfly kisses with her mama there, Sticking little white flowers all up in her hair. 'Walk me down the aisle, Daddy-it's just about time.' 'Does my wedding gown look pretty, Daddy? Daddy, don't cry' Oh, with all that I've done wrong, I must have done something right. To deserve her love every morning and butterfly kisses.*"

The good news—I was now safely parked at a rest stop.

The bad news—I was a lurching hot mess of man-snot and tears. I wasn't just crying; I was crying *hard* and sloppy. And I Didn't. Even. Have. A daughter.

Thanks to "Butterfly Kisses" by Bob Carlisle, from that moment on, I also knew two things for sure:

1) I was in deep trouble.
2) If God ever gave me a daughter, I was going to do every damn thing in my power to deserve her love and make the most of every minute of the years I have her.

The relationship between a father and a daughter is special. A father owns a sacred place in his daughter's heart forever, and a good father sees to it that this place is one of joy and fulfillment. This isn't the book that will explore the psychology or emotions of that dynamic. My point here is to stress how very important it is and how powerful the words and actions of a father are to his daughter. Let's explore *how*.

> BONUS: I know what you're thinking. "Maybe *he* cried, but clearly he has issues. I'm a tough guy." I'm completely fine with both assertions. But there's only one way to know for sure. Take the Butterfly challenge yourself: www.DadAthlon.com/Butterfly Let me know how you do.

The most valuable thing we have to give all our children, boys *and* girls, is time. There is no real shortcut to spending time with your kids, but there are ways to make the most *of* that time—things we can do, read, watch, play, write, and model for our kids.

Do

Dates

These don't need to be as big or formal as the name suggests. It *can* be as big as lunch or dinner once or twice a month to catch up and talk. But it can also be as little as sixty seconds before bed every night. The important factors are that they are regular, purposeful, and exclusive.

Regular

If you fail to plan, you plan to fail. Have you ever tracked how you spend your time over a day? Or reviewed where you spend your money? Were you surprised at how much of your time and money went to things you did not expect or value highly?

In a later chapter, we will discuss John C. Maxwell's comment that creating a budget is like telling your money where to go instead of wondering where it went. You don't necessarily have to meet that budget every month, but without a plan, you won't know how far off you were from what *you* decided was important.

Similarly, create an expectation for spending time with each of your kids. Even if only you know it, you can hold yourself accountable. If you can't remember the last time you had one-on-one time with your daughter, it's been too long.

Whether it's little things daily or large ones monthly, write it down and hold yourself to it. At least set a minimum. If you don't always hit those targets, be gentle with yourself. This is a marathon and not a sprint. Make up some time on the next mile if you need. But the value of creating some kind of expectation is that you *know* if you're falling behind the pace you set.

Purposeful

You don't need a formal game plan every time you spend alone time with your daughter. It's enough to know that this is *her* time right now, whether you're tucking her in or meeting her for coffee. Simply acknowledge that in your head, whether you've planned the moment or not. Sometimes you might have bigger plans too, and that's fine. And other times, opportunities will unexpectedly present themselves.

If you think of your time together as purposeful, you will behave that way with her, and she will sense it. Also, you will file those memories away more easily, giving your future self a treasure chest for the slideshow in your mind of the times you spent together.

Exclusive

There will always be moments you are with more than one of your kids—driving, participating in a family activity, watching a movie together, or having dinner. Those are also valuable activities to the health of your overall family. But don't use those as the "time with my daughter."

Whatever your schedule permits, be sure to set aside some time dedicated exclusively to your daughter. By this, I mean she is the only other human in your presence; ensure you focus your attention on her. That doesn't mean you can't spend this time also doing something else, but make sure you don't lose sight of the fact that *she* is the priority.

For example, "I need to rake the leaves—who can help? Oh, hey Jordan, come help me rake the leaves!" You might proudly check the "date box" for the week, but was that activity fun for her? Compare that to seven-year-old Jordan coming up to you asking if she can rake the leaves and jump in. In both instances, you and Jordan spend time with the leaves, but in the second example, she's having a great time. The focus is not your to-do list. But before you count an activity as a date, ask yourself if you're doing it for *her* or if she is doing it for *you*.

Regular Check-ins

Set aside a regular time depending on your schedules to check in with her. Doesn't have to be heavy topics. This could be over ice cream, coffee, lunch, or even a cocktail, depending on her age. How is she doing? What's on her mind? What is she proud of?

Quick Hits

Every night before bed—or first thing in the morning after waking up.

If you are a family of faith, one easy option to use is prayers before bed. These can be recited prayers, extemporaneous, or even sitting in silence together, pointing your hearts together in faith. There's no wrong here—whatever simple approach works for you.

Chose a word of the day, or maybe three, that describes the day that was. Or maybe over breakfast while getting ready for school—"What's your word going to be today?" It might be "tired," or "excited," or "nervous." Whatever the answer is, she knows you care what's on her mind, and you get insight into her day. Without something as simple as a word, some hard days may come and go, and dad will never know.

> Dad Hack. One great book to use for your daughters is *Let's Talk: Conversation Starters for Dads and Daughters*, by Michelle Watson Canfield, Ph.D. The author lays out many topics and questions for dads who want to connect with their daughters. Some issues are uncomfortable for dads, and navigating these waters without a map is scary. This book is an excellent resource. I've started this with both my daughters. While it was a little awkward going into the first date, that evaporated quickly as we got into some of the questions. It was silly and eye-opening for each of us, and each daughter later approached me asking when we could do the next one. Whenever a teenage girl comes up to her father and asks to repeat an event, you're doing something right. Thanks to this author for developing this book, which I highly recommend to dads of tween girls or older. You can find a link to this book at www.DadAthlon.com/Daughters

Social Media

Do not punt on this one. Get an account and connect with them. Even if you never post—for which she will likely thank you—at least have the account, so you're plugged into who she's hanging out with online. Be mindful that she may end up with several *other* accounts—the ones that do *not* have her parents as friends. Dealing with that is a different but important issue.

As she gets older, you may have to be mindful of what she's saying, or *wearing*, in her posts and engage accordingly. Every now and then, compliment her on something she posted. "I like the picture with your friends getting ice cream," or "Who is the girl, or *guy*, in the red shirt with you and your friends at the football game?" She knows she's important enough to you that you're paying attention to her, even outside your comfort zone.

Fight For Her

Fighting for her may not show up the way you think it will. We all know that a father will do anything for his little girl. All kinds of jokes and funny stories exist about dad shining his gun when the new boyfriend comes over. Or making idle, or *not* idle, threats conveying expectations about what time she should be home and where everyone's hands should remain all night. We all know that a father will fight anyone, especially a young man, to keep his little girl safe and healthy. But there is one special person a father must be willing and able to fight to protect his daughter. And that person is—his daughter.

This is perhaps less often the case before the teenage years, but a young woman needs to know, with your words and your actions, three things.

1) Boundaries and expectations exist.
2) They are in place for her physical and emotional well-being.
3) Anyone who crosses them will have to deal with you.

Before we get too deep in here, I am *not* saying that you should ever verbally or physically abuse your daughter or anyone else for that matter. Such behavior is the opposite of what I am saying and will have horrifying consequences both for her and your relationship.

I am saying a father should create and enforce clear boundaries, informed by what is in *her* best interest. Then stick by them even when she hates you for it in the moment. She may not appreciate it at the time, but underneath it all, she knows that you are pushing back on her because you love her.

Don't believe me? Spin the scenario around. What if she skittered all about town, staying out late, drinking, and sleeping with boys, and you are a "cool dad" who ignores that and leaves beer and liquor in the downstairs fridge when all her friends sleep over. You're the dad who doesn't lift a finger, but simply rationalizes this behavior as "kids will be kids."

What message do *you* think you are conveying to your daughter? Are you clearly communicating to her that she is valuable and precious beyond measure? Anything you do—or *don't* do—that allows her to miss that single point should cause you to question your role as her father.

This doesn't mean she *will* always make good decisions. Or that you ought to be *able* to prevent her from making poor ones. This is about demonstrating to her with crystal clarity that you *care* about her decisions because she deserves it. If the most important man in her life is passive or complicit about her decisions in the most formative years of her life, how do you think that is going to impact her future? Her happiness? Her self-worth? If her own father doesn't think she's important enough to avoid lousy decisions, why the hell would *she* think she is? Much less ever expect another man to think she is.

I once got into a heated argument with my daughter. While we didn't get to the sort of resolution where we agreed, and we barely even reached a place where we agreed to disagree, I managed to say to her exactly this: "Look! I love you enough to *always* fight for you. Even when the person I need to fight *is you!*" I'm sure she hated me at that moment. She wasn't capable of seeing the big picture the way I was. And I clearly lost the battle of Happy Peaceful Relationship With Your Daughter.

But I am okay trading that battle to win the larger war. The war that involves her knowing she is worth fighting for. Even when it's hard. *Especially* when it's hard. She may not understand that when she's fourteen or even eighteen, or possibly even twenty-four. And it's not important that she ever even recognizes it consciously, much less discusses it with you after ten years have passed. The point is that in creating and enforcing clear boundaries for her, you are communicating directly with her soul using your actions. She will be stronger, more confident, and expect more of herself because *she* knows she's worth it. In the long run, that will be its own silent and priceless reward.

Read

Books are a great way to connect with your daughters. A father can read *to* their little kids and read *with* older kids. Everyone knows that reading is important in general. A father can really seal the deal for a little girl if he teaches her to love reading by snuggling up with her before bed when she's tiny—or reading with her when she's little, or sharing books together when they're older. The fact that it's a useful life skill will be secondary to the feeling of warmth and importance she gets from undivided time with dad. This doesn't need to be a huge thing, but like the dates, make them regular.

As she gets older, you can simply ask her what she's reading, or if you see her on the couch, ask, "How's that book?" Or even "What's your favorite book?" Then *you* read it. Grab it from the library, or even better, listen to it on Audible so you can "read" it while you're driving to and from work or even mowing the lawn. Then ask her something about it: "Don't you think Daryl was a jerk when he said that?" or "What was the deal with Mandy's brother? Why did he freak out so much when she brought up their uncle?"

These examples are made up, but the point is to demonstrate that what she finds interesting is important to you *because* she finds it interesting. No need to go all fully geeked-out book club on her, unless that's her thing and your thing—in which case, by all means, *geek away!*

Ultimately, find threads of her life she finds interesting or compelling or heartbreaking and take hold of the same thread with her. Have long, in-depth discussions about them. Or simply observe, "Mandy's uncle is a turd." You do you, but do it with her. At least enough for her to know what matters to her matters to you.

> Bonus: While we are on the topic of books, an excellent one on developing a meaningful relationship with your successful and confident daughter is *Strong Fathers, Strong Daughters: 10 Secrets Every Father Should Know* by pediatrician and parenting expert Meg Meeker, M.D. This book is not one to read *with* your daughter but rather for you to get deeper insights into how she views both the world and her relationship with you. Some of my observations in this book are grounded in both my own experience and Dr. Meeker's rich and thoughtful treatment. I highly recommend it. She has many other great books as well, including *Boys Should be Boys*, which is also well worth reading.

Watch

Movies and TV shows provide another way to share time together when you and she are in a more passive mood. Movies out with just the two of you are always a special treat, but that might not always be possible and they eventually add up financially. You can always sit on the couch and pop a bag or three of popcorn and watch one of her favorites, a classic she hasn't seen before, or even a double feature where you each get to pick one. TV shows these days are great since you can either have a binge day-long date, or they work as your pre-baked date nights with her. Make them fun, chat with her about them, but don't ruin it with too much talk. Share the moment. Be in the moment. Laugh, cry, repeat.

> Dad Hack: Sometimes our kids want to watch a movie or show that may be above their maturity pay-grade—especially the youngest kids in a family! Whether you're selecting a movie to watch with your kids or merely determining if *Slaughter Porn 7* is, in fact, appropriate for your twelve-year-old to watch at her friend's birthday party, Common Sense Media is a great resource to gauge the appropriateness of many movies and TV shows as well as books and video games. https://www.commonsensemedia.org/.
>
> They provide not only their own target ages but also post what ages other parents and kids think as well as summaries of the plots and themes. They also provide category scores from one to five on language, violence, sex, and positive messages, among others. This is particularly handy when navigating worthwhile R-rated movies for younger teens. Perhaps you are okay with language but want to avoid sexy scenes.

> For example, when you look up *The Shawshank Redemption*, it observes:
>
> "Gritty prison tale has positive messages, lots of profanity."
>
> Common Sense says 16+,
> Parents say 15+
> Kids say 14+.
> Positive Messages: 4/5
> Language: 3/5
> Sex: 2/5
> Violence: 4/5

Can't figure out what to watch? Use one of your dates to put together a list of target movies and shows. Check out www.DadAthlon.com/Daughters for a list of suggestions.

Play

Imagination games: Play make-believe, tea parties, dress up, hide and seek, Simon says, charades. In today's world, devices are sapping our kids of their natural ability to use their creative imagination. Technology is cultivating little humans who live primarily in a passive, receptive mode. If we want kids to develop an actual proactive imagination, we need to make it a priority. Do what you can to let her know you're interested in her world, the one outside the device.

Games: These are similar to imagination games, but a time will come when tea time is passé. But your daughter's young and competitive mind is still hungry for time with you. There are always board games like Monopoly, Chess, and Sorry, or harder ones like Trivial Pursuit. Cards are always a good bet. Many easy-to-learn, fast-to-play games make it easy to play a quick hand or two over a few minutes *or* play to 500 over the long haul! Don't always let them win, but also don't always beat them. The goals are to have fun and build her confidence. Teach her how to play well, and you will teach her how to live well.

Sports: So far, we haven't even left the damn house. Your daughter may be into sports, or she may not. *You* may be into sports, or you may not. Either way, watching or playing sports is a great way to connect with her. She may grow to love a sport you do *because* you do, and it becomes your thing together. She may hate everything about traditional sports but loves a good hike or a bike ride. Get outside, get some sun, and sweat a little.

Try something new for both of you.

Attend a minor league ball game, go for a run together once a week, take a golf lesson together, and hit a bucket of balls for an hour on a weeknight after dinner. Take her fishing or hunting with you. If you're really brave, take a dance class with her at the local Arthur Murray studio. It may be horrifying and awful and hysterical. And she will probably love telling people that story about you for years. Her verbal story probably won't include the part about how deeply loved she felt because you were willing to embarrass yourself by doing something like that with her. But the one she tells herself certainly will. You decide if that trade is worth it.

Write

Most dads are typically not great at expressing their feelings in words. Many moms are fantastic at this, or at the very least way better than dad. But despite this, or perhaps because of it, the words we say to and about our daughters are even more important. Not more important than mom's words; they just carry more weight than all our other words put together.

She will receive words from you with an emotional heft and importance that few other people will get. The goal here is not to write a *lot* or even to write all the time. The goal is to express to her, in writing, from time to time, how much you love her and why she is special.

A while back, I read an article where someone suggested a father write a brief love-filled note to his daughter. Soon after writing the note, the dad forgot about it. Years later, as he helped her pack her room for a move, he noticed right in the nightstand top drawer, on top of all the other junk, was a folded, worn, and "velveteen" note—the letter he'd written years earlier. After writing it, he never thought of it again, but based on its appearance and location, she very well may have read it every single day since.

Do not underestimate the value and weight of your words. So write her notes. Silly. Serious. Short. Long. She will read them. She will be strengthened by them. She will be better because of them. But not if they never get written.

> Dad Hack: Tips for writing notes to your daughter. Use a pen, not a printer. Say something along the lines of, "I love you. I'm proud of you in ways and for things you don't even know you have. God has big plans for you, and I can't wait to see what they are. I am always here for you, no matter what. I love/admire your heart/laugh/empathy." Make it unique to your daughter. And if you happen to have more than one daughter, for the sake of all that is holy, write individualized letters to each of them—notes that could *only* be for them.

Model

Be the model of the person you want her to marry. Your grown daughter may get married or may not. But if a relationship or marriage is in her future, you are the first and most important template by which she will measure, or settle for, in her partner. Do you support and nurture your wife? Or berate her? What do you believe your daughter deserves in a husband or partner? Start today to live your life as a husband *exactly* according to that image.

You may not like every date she brings home or even the one who stays. But the outcome would be far worse if she felt in her bones that it was normal for a man to speak disrespectfully to his wife and the mother of his children.

Call *your* parents, stay connected to *your* siblings, help others. Be a good man, and she will not only grow in strength and love, but when it's time, she will find someone like you. She is watching.

Contemporary Christian artist Mark Schultz has a great song called "She Was Watching" that illustrates this beautifully. Take a listen when you visit www.DadAthlon.com/Daughters

Summary

We've explored the first of the "connecting" events in the DadAthlon—our daughters. Because dads don't have any direct experience of being a young woman, connecting with their daughters is both terrifying and incredibly important.

A daughter's relationship with her father is of singular importance in her life. If we want her to be healthy, happy, and fulfilled, we must take action early and often throughout her life to demonstrate our love and support.

Spending time that is regular, purposeful, and exclusive with your daughter is the first step. There are no shortcuts, but many options are available for enjoying this time together, including dates large and small, sharing books and movies, playing games or sports, writing brief, heartfelt notes to her, and modeling behavior she should both emulate and seek in a life partner.

Do

- Set aside purposeful time to spend with your daughter regularly. Schedule it on your calendar.
- Take advantage of tiny moments before bed or during breakfast to check in with a prayer or a word for the day.
- Create clear boundaries and enforce them firmly with love.
- Read a book with your daughter or read her favorite book and ask her about it.
- Make a list together of movies and TV shows to watch with your daughter and schedule regular time to watch them
- Learn a card game together or teach her.
- Write handwritten notes about how much you love her.
- Be an example of the person you would like her to marry.

Don't

- Let your busy-ness or discomfort become an excuse to delay spending time together.
- Rationalize that "she knows I love her."
- Assume she doesn't need you. Even if that is what she says.
- Behave in a way that allows your daughter to believe anything less than that she is valuable and precious beyond measure.

CHAPTER 3

CONNECTING WITH SONS

Every father should remember one day his son will follow his example, not his advice.

– Charles Kettering

I suck at skiing. Not surprisingly, we are not a big skiing family. We enjoy it from time to time, but it's never been our main thing. Back when we only had three kids, all under six, my in-laws bought a lake house in western New York not far from a small ski mountain. We'd visit every 4th of July but also sometimes during our February school break. We often signed the kids up for ski school in the mornings so they could learn. We adults could enjoy the mountain a bit on our own before grabbing lunch and hot chocolate. Then, we'd all head out together in the afternoon.

The first year we did this, it was Presidents Day Weekend. My daughters were six and four, and my older son was also four, his sister's twin. Like most boys, he has always been very energetic. And like most parents, we often worried that his need for excitement trumped his awareness of the potential risks. You might say that he'd often get out a little ahead of his skis.

On the mountain that first afternoon, he was with me and the girls were with my wife. We rode up the bunny hill lift together and had a few successful runs down as I held onto him. He kept asking me to let him go, telling me he was fine; being held was no fun. However, many people were on the mountain that day, and it seemed to me he hadn't quite mastered two rather desirable skills—turning and stopping.

On our fourth trip up the lift, he kept begging me to let him go this time. I'm not sure convinced is the right word, but he perhaps *annoyed* me into submission by then. When we got off the chair, and I tried to grab him to make sure he could turn and stop, he wriggled away and said, "Let me do it. I *can* do it!"

"*Fine!*" I shouted. "See what happens!"

To my embarrassed, guilty, and proud amazement, *I* was the one who saw what happened. He skied down the hill, turning a few times—not poetically, but with the measured control of a boy balancing the gleeful independence of the wind in his face with terror. I stood on the top of the hill, mouth agape, watching him get smaller and smaller. He reached the bottom of the bunny hill and came to a slow and steady pizza slice stop.

I learned two important lessons that day.

First, I was holding him back. What's more, I was the *only* thing holding him back. He was ready; the mountain was ready, and the equipment was ready. I and I alone prevented him from doing the one thing we were there to do.

Second, you often need to risk failure to learn and grow. It's not that I didn't believe in him. Based on the information I had at my disposal at the time, I had good reason to think he very well may have crashed and burned. The bigger issue is that I didn't balance it against the tradeoff.

No one wants to ski down a mountain ten times, always holding their dad's hand. A few times, sure. But the only way he could grow and learn was to jump from the safety net and do it on his own. That is scary for all involved. But whether he fell or made it down in one piece, the lesson was the same. Sometimes the best way we can support our kids is to let them support themselves. Learn from and bear the cost of the consequences. Then adjust.

Of course, many activities are great for all kids regardless of gender. But at the end of the day, boys and girls *are* different. Boys deal with the world and emotions differently and thus have different needs from their dad. As in the chapter about daughters, we will focus on actionable items to help fathers and sons connect.

It used to be the case that boys were supposed to be tough. Don't show emotions. Don't cry. Don't show weakness.

While boys and girls process anxieties and emotions differently, it is certainly not the case that boys lack that need altogether. We live in a complex world that is difficult for all kids. We know that social media pressures, increased rigor at school, and isolation during COVID pandemics don't help. It's no wonder that suicidal thoughts are rising among teens in general and especially young men. It is essential that we fathers create strong bonds with our boys so they know they are supported as they grow into strong, self-confident young men.

The basic framework of this chapter will be similar to the daughters' chapter with sections on do, read, watch, play, write and model. But some of the specifics look a little different for boys.

Do

Hangtime. Time with boys is different than time with girls. Perhaps with fewer words and more action. Wrestling, running, playing. Play catch in the yard, or go fishing, hunting or camping. While conversations with your daughter tend to have connection be the main event, checking in with your son is usually a side dish. "How's school?" or "So who's Kayla?" are words that get uttered not after you both sit down for an intense cup of coffee together, but maybe in the seventh inning of the game you're watching or on the 11th hole.

The bottom line? *Be there.* Engage. Do your best to do the things your kids want to do *with* them. They won't tell you how much it means to them, especially if they're over twelve. But it does.

Find out what he is interested in and plan time to do things together. What's his favorite team? Or band? Or comedian? Grab tickets and head out the door with him. Maybe he can invite one of his buddies. Many boys like video games. Head out for a day of just you and him at a giant arcade-like Dave & Buster's, where he can beat you in Zombie Apocalypse 4 while you kick his sorry butt in Skee Ball and Pop-a-Shot Basketball.

Talk with him about sex and expectations with women. Keep your radar up. This is obviously true with girls as well. But because boys are less likely to talk about their emotions and feel the cultural pressure to suck it up, they may feel they have less support. They may be less likely to seek help if they are anxious or stressed.

Add that to the fact that the suicide rate for boys is four times higher than girls, and the stakes are high. Be mindful of behavior changes. Mood swings. New friends. New habits. You're his dad; you know him. Trust your gut. There will be a time when you need to have a real sit-down how-are-you conversation when not hitting a bucket of balls or playing HORSE in the driveway. Mom's instincts are invaluable here, so be sure you stay on the same page, especially when he appears to be struggling.

Read

As with the girls, reading to *all* your kids when they're little is an easy and automatic way to bond with them. It also makes them feel safe, creates memories, and gives them a love of books.

As they get older, develop a menu of book options you think will appeal to your son. Discuss it with him. Have him pick a couple you both like and work through one. If you both agree that the one you're reading sucks, drop it and do another. Better to read one you both—but especially *he*—likes than to make this feel like a chore or homework to him.

From time to time, use the book as a springboard for conversation: "Where are you? Can you believe Tony did that? Isn't Mandy's uncle a turd? (Your sister thought so.)" Sneak those in while driving somewhere or playing catch in the yard. If you don't have time to read, you can listen to it on Audible. If you have long regular car rides with your son, listen to your book together in the car.

> Dad Hack: Audible: Busy dads often don't have as much time to read as they'd like. Audiobooks provide an easy way to consume books while also doing something else, especially driving or running. Owned by Amazon, Audible has an enormous catalog of books. It allows you to download and listen to audiobooks cheaply and easily. Learn more about how it works at www.DadAthlon.com/audible
>
> Want to kick it up a notch? Narrators talk slowly. Use the Audible app and listen to books at 1.25x or even 1.5x speed, which is closer to the pace of normal human speech. This also helps you get through the books in far less time. Listen during your commute or when exercising, and you can knock out a normal length book in a week or less without setting aside any additional time.

Watch

Similar to the girls, chilling on the couch and watching some stuff together is an easy and relaxing way to bond with your son. For movies, be sure to check off the classic comedies, sports films, and action movies. Get his thoughts on what movies he thinks *you* need to see. For example, Star Wars or Marvel movies are often a great place to start, and each have multiple sequels which make it easy to put movie selection on auto pilot if your son wants. But if you're looking for less conventional ideas or some deep cuts, check out www.DadAthlon.com/Sons for a list of suggestions.

Play

Like with daughters, it is important to play games and sports and be active. Encourage him to get out there. Teach him what you can. But the biggest thing is get off your ass. If the girls need you to be present and listen, the boys want you to be involved. They want you to see them out there, moving, running, competing, doing.

Coaching is a great way to bond with your son; you're teaching him something and creating positive memories. But only if you're not a jerk. If you are, that will have the total opposite outcome and be a rift in your relationship for years to come. Don't be the coach who plays his kids above all the better kids because you think he's better—or that he *ought* to be. But also don't be the coach who overcorrects and plays every other kid way more. Balance. Mr. Miyagi had it right. Not too much and not too little. Be encouraging, and be constructive, never angry.

Don't worry if you've never played a sport or don't know what you're doing, especially when they're little. Most leagues for younger kids just need some adult bodies for crowd control. You can do that. Google the rest. Pair up with a buddy who knows what he's doing and plan practices together over a beer.

I was a baseball kid and *never* played basketball beyond playing HORSE in my driveway. My son wanted to play on a team, and a buddy recruited me to coach. I bought a book for the basics and let my buddy organize practice and call the shots. I just followed his lead. In our case, the boys were seven; they'll never play professionally and are probably wiping their snot on their jerseys right now. There's only so much you can screw up. So relax and grab a whistle.

Let me let you in on a secret…the kids will never know you don't know what's going on.

Don't feel like coaching or learning something new? Play outside anyway, something silly with no formal rules. Just kick a ball around. Shoot hoops in the driveway or the park. Play catch in the backyard or head to the little league field with a bag of tennis balls to pitch to him.

> Dad Hack: Free Tennis Balls: Want a million free tennis balls to pitch to your kids? Head to your local tennis club. Once tennis balls lose their freshness, the club typically just tosses them. Head over and ask if they have any old or used tennis balls they'd like to get rid of. The first time I did that, I got a trash bag full!

Other ideas: Wii sports or active video games foster competition and are on his home turf.

Let him see *you* keeping active. Run, play squash, do a triathlon, whatever. Parents who sit on their asses all the time have kids who sit on their asses all the time.

Paintball/Laser Tag: This is the ultimate real-life hunt. Competition. Strategy. Shooting. And holy crap, will your quads burn for days! Take your son solo or have him grab a bunch of buddies as well. It's always good to get to know your son's pals too.

Speaking of which, get to know your son's friends and make sure they know you. Who our kids hang out with has enormous influence over who they become. So have his friends over. When in doubt, *you* be the one to have the movie night, pool party, or nerf gun war.

Scouts: Cub Scouting is a great way to bond with your young son. Scouting offers a wide variety of tailor-made activities. Yeah, it takes some time to prep, and some parents don't bother to participate. Don't be one of those guys—get your hands dirty and jump into the fray. Build birdhouses, make a fire, camp in the woods, hike, build rockets—together. Scouting is a great place to spend good quality non-device time with your impressionable son in the years he most wants to be with you. Don't lose sight of that.

Write

With boys, you can afford to be pithier than with your daughters. But it's still important to occasionally give them something concrete that reminds them you've got their back, you're proud of them, and you love them. A note in the lunch box. A sticky on the sock drawer. A random text. Maybe even a longer note. Just something they can go back to and look at when they doubt themselves or feel crappy. Remind them they are strong, even when they don't feel it.

Model

Be the man you want your son to grow into. Treat his mother with the utmost respect, even if you are no longer together. One of my favorite commercials from the 80s was a public service announcement about the Just Say No to drugs initiative. A dad walks into his son's room with a box and holds it in front of him. The dad opens the box, and it reveals drug paraphernalia. Accusingly, he asks his son, "Where did you learn to do this stuff?!?" For a few moments, tension hangs in the air in a cloud of sullen silence. Then finally, the son blurts out, "*You,* Dad! I learned it from watching *you!*" As the gob-smacked father recoils, the voiceover comes in, "Parents who use drugs have children who use drugs."

No one watches what you do, what you say, how you say it, and to whom more than your son. Your words and actions are their *main* script for life and manliness. It is a large responsibility, one you wear twenty-four hours a day, even when you're tired. Perhaps especially then.

Let him see you fail. Then get back up. Or tell him about a time you did, especially when or if he's having a hard time in school or a sport. He looks up to you and needs to know that the ideal is not perfection; it's progress.

No one is perfect, and that is not the goal. But when you screw up, own that too. Take responsibility for your mistakes. Respecting loved ones and relationships is more important than always being right or being tough. And spoiler alert—it is also harder. But worth it.

If you're wrong or speak angrily to your son or his siblings, be sure you loop back afterward to own your part. Wounds left untreated become infected. Period. And you are the adult.

You may get into arguments with mom, and it's okay for him to see that, as long as it is, at least eventually, respectful. How he sees *you* treat *his* mother, as well as other women you interact with, will become the blueprint he uses. Know that.

If you say or do something you regret in front of him, *fix* it in front of him. Apologize and own it and be a man in front of him. Being a man doesn't mean never making mistakes or being some macho tough guy. It means owning your mistakes, admitting you ought to have done better, then actually following through.

Summary

While boys have many of the same needs as girls regarding feeling loved and supported, we need to communicate this to them differently. Books, movies, and TV shows are one way to connect, though very different from the ones your daughters will enjoy.

Sons need to get their energy out, and many fun, cool and easy options are available to help you bond with each other actively, including sports, competing, and games. So whether you choose casual activities in the yard, coaching a team, or leading a Cub Scout pack, it's important for dads to actively engage with their son's activities.

A son will emulate everything his father does—good and bad. Therefore, it is critical to model good behavior in living, failing, learning, and speaking. Especially important here is treating your spouse well.

Do

- Be the man you want your son to grow into.
- Let him see you make mistakes, take responsibility, and fix them.
- Plan time with your son doing active events like concerts, arcades, axe-throwing, or laser tag.
- Make a list of kickass movies, old and new, to watch together.
- Get actively involved in coaching, scouts, or whatever activity he's interested in.
- Get to know his friends.
- Tell him he's awesome in writing or in person.
- Check-in and have deeper, more meaningful conversations when necessary.

Don't

- ➤ Assume he's fine because he hasn't said anything is bothering him.
- ➤ Pretend you're perfect.
- ➤ Disrespect his mother.
- ➤ Let mom have all the hard conversations.

CHAPTER 4

CONNECTING WITH MOM

> One of the greatest things a father can do for his children is to love their mother.
>
> – Howard W. Hunter

I love Tom Hanks. I know—very bold statement. I obviously don't know the man, but I have certainly appreciated his work over the years ranging from *Bosom Buddies* to *Forest Gump* to *Philadelphia* and *Toy Story*—hell, I even liked *Joe Versus the Volcano*!

But both as a father and as a man, one role that sticks with me most is from the movie *Castaway*, where he plays Chunk Noland, a FedEx manager. His plane crashes in the middle of the ocean, stranding him on an island for several years, completely isolated. With nothing more than nature, a few FedEx packages, and his own grit, Chuck masters the art of survival in the most challenging environment.

The movie does a great job of showing his early efforts stumbling about, trying to make fire or a shelter. He exerts enormous physical and psychological effort to succeed at an otherwise modest goal—fire—something folks *not* on an island take for granted every day. From his early struggles and failures, we flash forward several years to an image of a fish being deftly speared from a distance of twenty yards. With effort and grit, he understood that in order to survive, he would have to push well beyond his comfort zone.

I don't know about you, but my wife and I often tell my kids that they need to push themselves beyond their comfort zones to find true success in life, sports, or school. Sit at the table where you don't know anyone, take the tougher class, sign up for the play even though none of your buddies do.

"Tough talk, Dad, but do you ever push yourself out of your own comfort zone?" For most of my life, my answer was someplace between never and not enough.

Supporting, understanding, and empathizing with the mother of your children is clearly important. But how to do this best is often a very uncomfortable proposition for men.

Most fathers, it turns out, are men.

We all want to support our wives as much as possible. Many times though, the spirit may be willing, but the flesh is weak. We either don't know what to do or, worse, know damn well and passively allow her to do the heaviest lifting, all while rationalizing reasons why that makes sense.

Chuck Noland needed to push himself well outside of his comfort zone to stay alive.

The stakes are similar. I am not suggesting that our wives are as challenging and difficult as a desert island—rather, like survival, that our kids and marriages are worth *all* our best efforts. Kids are parented better when they are parented together. We all know parenting well is incredibly hard and requires continuous mutual support from those closest to us. That begins and ends with a healthy relationship with their mom.

Doing that well is often outside our comfort zone, but it doesn't need to be. In this chapter, we'll explore a few simple strategies to bring this critical mission inside our comfort zone.

Let's begin with a simple thought experiment for reflection.

Two friends of yours from college, Ken and Brian, go into business together as partners developing software. They get off to a strong start, hire a few employees, and have initial success.

As the business grows, they need to develop skills around bookkeeping, management, and strategic planning. Ken took classes, managed the team, organized the meetings, and so on. Brian was there to help, and anytime Ken asked him to do something, he did it. Sometimes Brian even worked extra hours to pitch in during the busy season.

Both owned the business, but Ken owned the decisions and the game plan in a way that Brian did not.

Who is behaving like an owner, and who is behaving like an employee? If you were a venture capitalist, which guy would you hire. Why?

Let's get real. If your family were a business, would you and your wife be co-owners? Would one of you be an employee? Are there aspects of your family life or kids' care that just happen, and you don't even know what you don't know?

...the doctors' names and numbers?
...the grade on the last algebra test?
...the sleepover that went bad?
...which friend turned into a bitch?
...what tampons your daughter needs?

What if someone offered you $10,000 right now to answer one specific question about your family? But if you get it wrong, you lose $10,000. And *only* you or your wife can answer with no help from the other. Who do you think should answer?

If your wife received the same offer, do you think she'd call you? What if the question were: "What is the one thing my wife needs in the world more than anything?"

These questions are not accusatory. But they *are* designed to push you out of your comfort zone a bit.

You can't say I didn't warn you.

As you reflect on those questions, are you behaving like a co-owner in the business of your family? Anticipating needs and planning accordingly?

But if you wanted your wife to answer the $10,000 question, maybe it's worth exploring why. Is it hard to understand how she may sometimes feel a little like Ken?

It's great that Ken can ask Brian to do anything, and he does it. But maybe what Ken sometimes needs is help *with*, or a break *from*, making certain decisions.

Or maybe Ken needs to know that, although they are co-owners, Brian truly understands all the heavy lifting that Ken does.

One of the most important roles of dad is to support mom. Prior generations of men may have thought, "I don't need to 'help' at home. I'm the one who brings home the bacon."

In today's busy world, that is often not true and certainly not sufficient to do dad-ness right. Yep, providing is *one* category of events in the DadAthlon, but it is worth noting, mom likely does that too, and there is more to be done than *just* provide.

You probably already know that since you're reading this book. We all need support, and mom needs to know you are a co-owner, not just a taller kid with louder toys. Making her feel safe, supported, and secure requires more effort than direct deposit and lawn skills.

When you fully support your wife and are co-owners of the family business, you will be a happier couple. You will also have kids who will feel loved, supported, and fulfilled as they navigate this crazy world. Of course, this will not inoculate you from the world's troubles or from problems with each other. And certainly not with your kids. But when you and your wife are proactive in this together, you will be in *much better shape* to handle anything the world throws at you.

This certainly doesn't mean single moms or dads, or other guardians cannot parent effectively. But if you need to carry a dozen forty-pound bags across a football field, would you prefer to do that alone or with a supportive partner? Some trips you can do together; others may be a solo trip while your spouse or partner takes a well-needed break. The bottom line is that with the support of a partner, it is easier for *both* people than it would be for either alone.

Connecting effectively with your kids' mom is a critical event in the Dadathlon. Three simple ways to achieve this are to communicate well, clarify roles, and show her with actions.

Communicate Well

The most important thing parents can do is to ensure they are on the same page. The only effective way to do that is to communicate.

"But what the hell does that *look* like? I talk to my wife every day. But we still get into it and have trouble managing everything without regularly wanting to strangle each other!"

The secret is to communicate smarter, not harder. And for many men, the tallest part of that order is to truly listen.

We've all been there—we see a problem, and we want to fix it. We jump to solutions before she's even done processing the emotions of the problem. Our instinct with wives and children is to make the discomfort stop immediately. When we have done so, we have fixed the situation.

Next.

Maybe I'm overstating that a bit. You tell me. Either way, to listen to our wives effectively, we need to push outside our comfort zone. Like Tom Hanks early in Castaway, *how* we need to listen is not our natural instinct, but we can get there if we're committed.

Listen, don't solve. At least at first. Have you ever been in a facilitated consultation discussion at work? People want to jump straight to the solution, but they *first* need clarity around identifying and understanding the problem.

What did you do the last time your car didn't start? Did you automatically replace the battery? Of course not. It could be the battery, but maybe it's the starter or the alternator. First, you, or your mechanic, must thoroughly diagnose the underlying issue. This requires a deeper understanding of both the car and the circumstances. It makes sense when it's a car, but it's much harder to do thoughtfully with our loved ones.

Please note, I am not suggesting that our wives are like cars. Instead, the takeaway from that analogy is that time spent truly understanding the circumstances of a challenging situation makes it easier to handle difficulties that arise. That may not be your strength when it comes to people, but then again, that's why you're reading this chapter. Right?

Men and women are different. We all know that. It's not that men are unable to listen; it's *how* we typically listen that is different from what our wives need.

So when a difficult situation arises, how, specifically, should you listen? Follow these three simple steps.

FSA: **F**ocus. **S**hut up. **A**sk.

1) Focus. Put your damn phone down. Shut the TV off. Give her your undivided attention.
2) Shut Up. When you want to jump in, don't. This is the hardest one for me.
3) Ask simple open-ended questions, invite more clarity, and demonstrate curiosity. Some examples are:
    a. How did that make you feel?
    b. Tell me more about that.
    c. What do you think that means?

Fight the temptation to jump to answers or solutions. This may not be easy or come naturally to most of us, but it's important to listen to her in the way that she needs to be heard. Try to understand her perception of the problem. Why she thinks it's bad—which may be different from your take—and how it makes her feel. Like anything, this is a skill that takes practice. When in doubt, start with the three questions above.

Also, when something is on *your* mind, share it with her. No one wins if you always keep your concerns to yourself.

Clarify Roles

There is a lot to do in a busy family. That doesn't mean you both need to do everything. Dividing up roles is not only a good idea; it is a necessary one. But you do need to know what the roles are. It is essential to know and fully understand what she is doing and its importance—just as you want her to understand what *you* are doing and why it's important.

One big source of stress in many marriages, mine included, is a lack of clarity about who does what and who *owns* what. By owns, I don't mean stuff, but areas of responsibility within the household. Simply sitting down one day to hash that out is the simplest, most effective way to address this need.

Clarify roles and expectations, such as I lead this, and you drive that. Renegotiate as needed. Lawn, school, doctors, chores—lay them all on the table. Don't just assume this and that is *her* area, especially if your reason is that's just the way it's always been.

Ownership. If she feels like *she* alone owns everything, *you* become one of the kids. She becomes stressed. Resentment and or anger follow. The kids suffer.

Make a list of all the stuff that needs to be done, including general areas like doctors or finances, and specifics such as who will drive kids to appointments or manage budget and plan for college.

Determine who feels like they own it now. Look at the list. For categories where you each think there is not a problem, no need to really discuss further. Focus on the areas where one or both of you are not feeling clear or supported.

Be sure to factor in knowledge and time. One of you may be a better fit than the other because you know more about the car or the bills or the medical needs. As for time, you should consider both how *much* time is required for certain tasks as well as if there is a specific time of day or the week it needs to be done, which may better fit someone's schedule.

The important part isn't that you both conform to some perfect objective balance. What's important is that you agree and are clear on whatever balance you both come up with. It is especially important to re-clarify that you're on the same page following large life events. The birth of a child, a job change, or new demands within a category—such as kids starting high school—can throw off what used to be a well-balanced plan. Even a global pandemic throws a wrench into the works!

Determine who is the lead in which areas and what the other person's support role looks like. Mom may be the lead on managing health and doctors but may need to have you take someone to an appointment when she has a conflict. You may both end up with a conflict you have to work out, but that is different from simply assuming mom will take care of it. If you've already discussed it and have committed to helping out when she asks, you're both on the same page. That reduces the chances one of you will feel resentment or abandonment. Together you can brainstorm another solution. Maybe that means you call the doctor to reschedule the appointment for a time you can drive.

Clarifying roles might take some time, but it doesn't have to feel like a giant crappy project. Combine it with something enjoyable—a nice dinner or a few cocktails on the back patio on a summer evening. Or break the discussion down into a few smaller sessions over coffee or lunch during the week.

Once you've clarified the starting point, it's a good idea to ensure you stay on the same page with regular meetings. My wife and I sit down at Dunkin' every other Saturday to do a quick review of upcoming activities and commitments. We'll also cover family priorities—both fun, like vacations and movie nights, and business, like college applications or baseball practice transportation.

One benefit of this strategy is verifying we are on the same page and feeling good about that. But the best value from these check-ins is the peace of mind from solving the logistics for the next two weeks. It takes a plan to ensure everyone gets to where they need to be and does everything they need to do. There is nothing worse than realizing on Wednesday at 4:30 pm that you need to get each of your kids to three *different* places at 5:00 pm. But if you saw that coming over coffee on Saturday, you have plenty of time to plan for it.

On top of all that, it's nice to bake in regular time with your wife whether you discuss managing the family or not. As an added bonus, your children will clearly see the following.

1) You two are a team.
2) Life is hard and requires effort to do it well.
3) You enjoy each other's company.

Bonus: If you are really committed to this planning idea, you might even consider setting aside a full day or weekend for a couple's annual planning retreat developed by The ONE Thing. Some are in person, and others are online. These retreats provide a great way to connect with each other and connect with your goals and values as a family. Plus, you'll map out a plan to get there. Check out www.DadAthlon.com/Mom for more info as well as a link to this resource.

Show Her With Actions

How does your wife like to feel love? Not everyone prefers to receive love in the same way, which sometimes creates a disconnect between couples. This is especially true if one expresses his or her love the way *he or she* prefers, which may be different than the way the spouse prefers.

The 5 Love Languages is a book by Gary Chapman that explores this topic. It is a quick read, and the website is also worth exploring. On the website, you and your wife can each take a quiz to better understand your preferred love language. Once you see your results, share with your spouse and see if the information resonated with both of you. In a nutshell, the five love languages are—words of affirmation, quality time, receiving gifts, acts of service, and physical touch.

Whether you read the book or not, it might be useful to have a discussion with your wife about which of these she appreciates most. Then you can better express your love for her in the way she needs most. Find a link to their free quiz at www.DadAthlon.com/Mom.

You can even download an app where you can take the quiz and enable "love nudges" to stay connected to each other in ways consistent with how you each need to express and experience love. Remember, giving and receiving love goes both ways.

Finally, be straight with her about what's working for you and what your needs are. You guys are a team and work best as a team, supporting each other. Do everything you can to appreciate, validate and support her. But also be honest with her about when you need something, whether it's your own validation from time to time or just a break.

Fill Her Cup

We are all very busy. Sometimes it's easy to get so lost in the weeds of daily needs that we forget to fully see and *appreciate* all we have to be grateful for. This can be especially true at home.

Mom does a lot. It's as simple as that. And like anyone, she needs an occasional attagirl from the people who matter most, and that starts with you. Tell her you *see* what she's doing, know it's *hard*, and are *thankful* for everything she's doing.

The more specific, the better. Compare the following two statements:

"I really appreciate everything you do to keep this family running." It is simple and effective, can be used without an example, and beats the snot out of never saying anything.

But compare that to "I know what a pain it must have been to cancel that work meeting so you could take junior to the doctor, especially because your job has been super busy lately. I really appreciate you doing that."

While either one works well, the specifics in the second example demonstrate not only appreciation but understanding.

Sometimes opportunities like the above arise out of the blue. It is also important to intentionally schedule time to connect. Connecting doesn't always have to happen during a problem or crisis. Instead, sometimes it is meaningful to grab a nice dinner or coffee and sincerely ask, "How *are* you?" or, "What's stressing you out?"

Even better would be if you already had an idea in mind of what she needs. Then you can ask if that is something you can do to help. For example, "I know you have that big presentation on Wednesday. Is there anything I can do to help this week go well for you?" Whether she says yes or no, she will appreciate the fact that you noticed, cared, and offered support.

Sometimes little things can go a long way. Post-it notes can be powerful in a way that is disproportionate to their size. Try writing, "Thanks for the coffee," "You look cute today," or maybe something saucier. Texts are also a quick and easy option. Small gestures like that show her you're thinking of her. They let her know you love her and that she is important to you and the family.

In relationships and life, it's been my experience that multiple small things over time often outweigh the result of any great or grandiose effort.

Special Events

The little things do matter. But special days are special for a reason. Her birthday, Mother's Day, your anniversary, and holidays are nice opportunities to appreciate and validate her.

Get ahead of them—don't wait until the day before or the morning of. Set aside some time now to brainstorm a few ideas in advance, so you have them at the ready as the day approaches. Enter them into your calendar a week or two before her special day, and make sure they repeat annually so you won't lose track of those cool ideas.

Do your best to personalize it to what her needs might be. Encourage her to take time away to recharge—plan a weekend or day for her to get away with her friends. Or purchase a subscription box related to her favorite hobby—millions of great subscription box ideas are available, find one that is perfect for her. Cards and flowers are great, but the more your gift demonstrates your genuine and specific appreciation of all that she is, the better. She deserves it.

Validate

She kicks ass. Respect her *actively* in front of the kids. This doesn't mean merely not disrespecting her. Proactively give her shout-outs in front of the kids, her friends, or your friends. Try saying things like, "Didn't your mom do a great job with…." or "Your mom kicks ass…." or "You should have seen how well Sarah handled that…."

Don't conspire with your kids behind mom's back—unless it is a surprise *for* her. "Don't tell your mother…" is a dangerous sentence. Asking the kids to keep secrets, even simple or innocent things like ice cream or earrings, can create an unhealthy situation. That small expectation that you and your wife are anything other than on the same page can damage your relationship with your wife as well as how your children perceive your relationship.

If you are divorced or separated, this dynamic can be very challenging. I don't have any first-hand experience with this, and every situation is uniquely fraught with difficulty. As a general principle, it's not fair to your children to put them between you and your ex-wife in any way, shape, or form. They almost certainly see the situation more clearly than you think. Whether they're caught in the middle trying to fix things, preventing arguments or taking advantage of any daylight between you two, they will pay the emotional and psychological toll unless adults actively prevent it. You and your ex-wife need to be the adults. You don't need to agree, and you don't need to like it or each other, but you need to be consistent with the kids. Screwing that up doesn't harm your ex-wife; it harms your kids.

If you're a single dad, beyond parenting consistently, how do you treat women who aren't the mother of your children? Dating many, sleeping with some, kids waking up to see a different one every couple of weeks? What are you communicating to your sons? What are you communicating to your *daughters*? Live your life, but make damn sure you are crystal clear that you have excellent answers to these questions as you determine what that new life looks like for you. Your sons and daughters will take the cues for their lives from your behaviors whether you want them to or not. Behave accordingly.

Summary

Parenting is a hard job. When you and your wife are on the same page and supporting each other, better outcomes follow for the kids and the adults.

Thoughtfully supporting your wife is sometimes outside your comfort zone. Three simple strategies are helpful to connect with her.

Communicate well by listening before problem-solving—use FSA (Focus, Shut Up, Ask).

Clarify roles to efficiently get things done, ensure you're both on the same page, and prevent resentment.

Show her your love by taking action. Determine what she needs and ensure you regularly fill her cup and demonstrate your appreciation.

Separated dads need to work harder to ensure kids don't become collateral damage in an adult war.

Do

- Set up a time to clarify your roles, preferably over coffee, cocktails, or dinner.
- Put special days in your calendar a week in advance.
- Fill her cup regularly with appreciation and validation.
- Actively seek ways to recharge her batteries, with *and* without you.
- Brag about her publicly, especially in front of your kids.
- Schedule regular time with her to manage the family, but make it enjoyable.
- Allow her to support *you*.

Don't

- Disrespect her at all, and especially in front of the kids.
- Have secrets with the kids from her, unless it is a surprise *for* her.
- Complain about her publicly.
- Keep your own needs secret.
- Behave like you're an extra kid.

PART 2
DOING MORE - PROVIDING

If you don't know where you are going, you will probably end up somewhere else.

— Laurence J. Peter

Perhaps no aspect of fatherhood creates more stress in a man than the responsibility of providing for his family. It can be logistically difficult to manage and often comes with an unhealthy serving of comparisons. Some of these might include:

> "I want to give my kids more opportunities and nicer things than I had."

> "I promised my father-in-law his daughter and grandkids would want for nothing."

> "My brother/sister/in-laws are so much more successful."

> "My friends and neighbors go on fancy vacations way more than we do."

It is challenging these days to bring home the bacon in a way that adequately keeps these comparisons at bay. Time and dollars are limited resources, but they are also dynamic—they will move in some direction no matter what. Dads need to *actively* manage, steer and balance both or risk passively sacrificing the goals they have for their families. That begins with figuring out what those goals are, then mapping out the balanced journey we take to achieve them.

Later in the book, we'll explore balancing perspectives when discussing health, joy and wisdom in Part 3. As we begin Part 2, though, we'll walk through some actionable plans on making it all happen.

In Chapter 5, we'll cover simple strategies on effective execution—how to make auto-pilot progress on the goals we decide are most important. Chapters 6 and 7 focus on the bacon itself—dollars. Chapter 6 focuses on defense—protecting the money going out the door. Chapter 7 uses that momentum to build a stronger offense—increasing the money coming in the door.

In each chapter, we'll cover a few fundamental principles and include specific actions that help dads *provide* more effectively for those they love the most.

CHAPTER 5

EXECUTION

> We are what we repeatedly do. Excellence, then, is not an act, but a habit.
>
> – Will Durant (summarizing Aristotle)

A while back, I was in crappy shape. I was a runner when I was a kid, but a full-time job and four very young kids made it hard to find time to do much of anything, much less muster the energy to decide what that anything should be!

Well, that's what I told myself anyway. I was gaining weight, needing new clothes, and starting to hear pleas from my knees to give them a break from the extra load I was asking them to carry.

Every time I started exercising, I stuck with it for a few days. Maybe even a week. But then, one day, I'd wake up and convince myself I deserved an extra twenty minutes of sleep. Then another snooze. I'd think, "Now I don't have time to run anyway, so I'll just sleep for another fifteen minutes then get up to get the kids ready for school."

Rinse. Repeat. Running initiative over.

Then one day, in a burst of foolish inspiration, I told my wife I wanted to run a marathon. It's something I always had on my bucket list, and I figured it would be better to knock it out before I turned forty. I found a book online that mapped out eighteen weeks of training to get me from 2 miles to 26.2.

I printed the planner out, and it didn't look all *that* daunting. I "only" had to run four days a week. The three runs during the week were short, medium, short, then a long run on the weekend, book-ended by a rest day on either side. No sweat.

Turned out it was damn hard after all. But not the running part.

Stay with me—I know you've heard this kind of stuff before, but my take is different.

The first week was cake. Then by week two, the novelty started to wear off a bit. My schedule during days and evenings was always choppy, so the only time of day I could consistently dedicate to running was first thing. So mid-way through week two, I had a problem. I used to tell myself I deserved a little extra sleep, and up until that point, there was no rebuttal.

Now I had a new part of my brain saying, "You idiot. You're running a marathon, and if you keep skipping days, you'll fall behind and won't be able to catch up." To which the first voice in my head replied to no one in particular, "Hey, who brought the asshole?"

The marathon circled on the calendar was sixteen weeks and three days away. Seeing the plan between then and now laid out so clearly, *and* telling my wife and kids I was doing this made it hard to listen to Snooze-man—even if it was super annoying to listen to Run-man.

Sure I might skip a day here or there. But I had to make it up on one of the three off days. Since two off days were on either side of the long run, I could only reschedule one run once per week.

Damn.

Over time, though, getting up and going for a run became my default. Like a massive planet's gravitational pull, my goal and plan had a gravitational pull that got me out of bed before Snooze-man was even awake.

Over the subsequent weeks and months, it was often tough on my body and mind. But once I had this habit installed and on auto-pilot, it way easier for me to complete the training. I ended up finishing the marathon a few minutes under my goal time and felt great about my accomplishment.

Wow, that was a quick finish to the story.

That's because the story doesn't end there. The day after the marathon, I didn't run. After all, it's good to give your body a break to recuperate. That seems responsible.

On Monday, I said that same thing, which was probably true-ish.

Tuesday came, and I really *could* have gone on a quick run, but Snooze-man was up early too and whispered, "You deserve an extra 20 minutes of sleep, so…."

Snooze-man is a sneaky son of a bitch. He patiently waited four months until I *didn't* have a goal with a plan in place. The second I didn't, there was no one to argue with him when the alarm went off.

Six months went by like that, and I didn't run. Once.

I thought for sure I had installed my run habit forever because I did it every day for four months, and it got easier and easier to get out of bed. But without the gravitation pull of my goal and plan pulling my lazy ass out of bed, Snooze-man won.

Once I accomplished my goal, the Death Star blew up Alderaan, and I didn't even know it. I gained back most of the weight I lost and once again began fielding complaints from my exasperated and overburdened knees.

The following year. I decided to run a 5K with my kids. I couldn't show up fat and lazy. With a goal once again in place, I told myself I needed to run four times a week to get in shape for the race. A clear picture of that race with a plan, as simple as it was, kicked Snooze-man to the curb, and I re-installed my habit just like before.

That clear goal looming *publicly* in front of me was a valuable motivator to get off my butt and create the healthy habits I wanted.

My Lessons

1) Goals have gravity. They pull you toward them even when you don't realize it. When you lack goals of your own, everyone else's goals will pull you toward theirs.
2) Plans create clarity. Even simple plans give you clarity on what to do in the moment of choice, whether that's right when you wake up, after work or sometime in between. Plans remove the extra barrier of having to figure out what to do.
3) Habits are laziness vaccines. Habits require effort to install but much less to maintain. Once in place, a good habit will put you on auto-pilot, heading toward your goal. Then you can stack another on top of it to fast-track it or pick your next goal and install a habit that works *that* plan.

Habits work *best* when they are part of a plan that aligns with a clear goal. I *thought* I had the running habit baked after the marathon, and I could afford to take a few days off. But, as I mentioned above, Snooze-man is a savvy son of a bitch.

This is not to say it is impossible to create good or useful habits outside of goals. But selecting habits that support your chosen goals…

1) will *align* with what you say is important in your life,
2) are more *likely to stick* if skipping them jeopardizes those important goals, and
3) will, in time, ensure the heavy lifting of hitting your goals will be on *auto-pilot*.

Here's the catch, and this was for me the hardest part—*one at a time*. Technically, the hard part isn't picking the one thing. And it's not even creating a plan or doing it every day. It's allowing yourself *not* to worry about all the other stuff. Yet.

Sure, other things need to get done, but *focus* on installing the first thing first. Get it working. *Then* install the second thing. Get it working. If a camera is trying to focus on more than one thing, it is focusing on neither.

In *The Total Money Makeover*, financial author Dave Ramsey talks about the best way to get out of debt if you owe to various creditors. Make the smallest possible payments to everyone, except for your lowest balance. You *focus* all remaining available dollars on the lowest balance so that you pay it off first. Then once that is done, focus on the second-lowest balance, creating a debt snowball that grows bigger as you pay off each balance.

Similarly, focus on one habit until it is automatic, then move on to the next one, creating a habit snowball. It requires a lot less effort to maintain a habit once installed than to create a new one.

Create habits one at a time. When you stack new habits onto those already installed, their combined energy will snowball into awesomeness.

There are three principles of developing habits that correlate with goal achievement and long-term success. I like to express them as equations – well technically, *in*equations:

Clear > Squishy
Small > Big
Consistent > Choppy

Clear > Squishy

In his *7 Habits of Highly Effective People*, Stephen Covey's very first habit is to begin with the end in mind. If we are aiming at nothing in life, we will get it every time. That sounds self-evident, but it's incredible how many people don't do that.

Picture the last time you were at the airport. You have your ticket in hand, and they are boarding your flight. But when they call you to board, the destination on the gate now says Someplace, USA.

Do you board the plane?

Of course not! You have a clear destination in mind, so if the plane isn't going there, you don't get on. You check all the gates until you find the plane going to the specific location on your ticket.

Life itself is a far more essential plane ride. Oddly, though, most folks simply board the Someplace, USA flight.

In the airport, you have a crystal-clear picture of your destination. When the plane doesn't match that, you take action.

The difference in life is that we often do *not* have any clear destinations. We have a general sense of "not here" combined with "hopefully better."

Imagine you are booking your next family vacation with a travel agent. They ask where you want to go. How confident would you be that the agent could create a great vacation for you and your family if your only guidance to them were "not here" and "hopefully better?"

Getting clarity is not as daunting as you fear it is. You probably already have a general sense of what you want. You know what church to attend; you just need clarity on which pew is best for you. As you move through this book, some ideas might dawn on you in the following categories.

- Pay off debt
- Connect with your daughter or son
- Save for college
- Plan a vacation
- Lose twenty pounds

These general ideas find clarity when you introduce results, values, and dates. Compare the list above to the following:

- Pay off Visa credit card balance of $2,700 by July 1.
- Enjoy planned one-on-one time every month with each of my two kids through the end of the school year.
- Save $3000 for college by December 31.

➢ Plan and book a two-week beach vacation in July of next year by November 1.
➢ Weigh 185 by June 1.

With outcomes and timeframes defined, you can achieve Ninja-level clarity by creating accountability. When someone else knows what you're supposed to be doing, *not* doing it in front of them can be a powerful motivator. The more public, the better—shame can be a powerful motivator! Share your goal with your wife, your kids, your buddies, or your boss.

> Dad Hack: Putting money where your mouth is. Are you *really* serious about accountability? Confident you can do it? Interested in kicking it up a notch? While shame can be a powerful motivator, dollars can really make things move! Several websites motivate you to hit your goal by putting your own money on the line if you don't achieve it. Many are in the fitness and weight loss space, but not all of them. Hit your goal and get your money back, plus more. Miss your goal and lose the money you put up. You are literally putting your money where your mouth is. Here are a few worth checking out:
>
> www.waybetter.com: Fitness and weight-related. DietBet and StepBet live under this brand, and you bet money to hit certain weight or activity goals over two to six weeks.
>
> www.stickk.com: Broader than fitness only. Create any goal you want to be customized using a Commitment Contract. Non-fitness examples include "Work eight hours per week on future income stream," "Recharge or Family Time once a week," and "Write or edit one blog post per week."

> www.beeminder.com: You can set any type of goal. This app provides daily prompts to enter progress and tracks the data on detailed graphs. Go off the rails, and your credit card is charged.

Small > Big

Clarity *begins* with large giant goals like these, but it doesn't end there. It is certainly good to have a clear vision of what you want your life to look like in three, five, and ten years. But for our purposes, we don't need to flesh out a large life-long three-dimensional plan.

In some cases, we may need to break down long-term goals into smaller components. For others, it's enough to simply identify a destination and start walking in that direction. Pick one goal and *only one* to focus on, where we can both measure progress and build habits. Then put in place a simple plan where the habits you install move you toward that goal.

Sure, at some point, you'll need to save $200,000 to get your kids through college. But for now, break that financial goal down into smaller chunks and start there, focusing only on the first one. Start with the next six or twelve months and a way more doable number like $2,000 or $3,000. Focus on that. Build habits that point toward that. Measure your progress in relation to that.

Like training for the 5K, having a committed date and amount will ensure you make up for lost runs if you skip a day—*especially* if you have an accountability partner. At the end of six months, the little habits you've built to hit your mini-goal will set the table for your bigger, more effective habits to follow.

An accumulation of small things is stickier and has longer-lasting consequences than big irregular ones. This applies not only to the goals but also to the habits you select. As we will explore in the next section, the most essential aspect of habit formation is consistency. The larger a habit is, the harder it will be to remain consistent. This is especially true when we are first trying to build a habit. As you begin to select daily routines that support your goal, you may be tempted to swing big—"I will run every day for 40 minutes."

Setting a lower bar, one you can achieve every single day with no excuses, will serve you better. Anything above that will be gravy.

Thirty consecutive days—even though many days may be only five minutes—will pay much better dividends than ten days of larger inconsistent effort. This brings us to our final inequation.

Consistent > Choppy

"Some things you have to do every day. Eating seven apples on Saturday night instead of one a day just isn't going to get the job done." –Jim Rohn

An accumulation of small habits executed *consistently* over time is both more sustainable and predictive of success than a giant pile of effort dumped out on the floor one day. It makes sense when you say it that way, but we often forget that in life's real moments.

Comedian Jerry Seinfeld committed to writing a joke a day every day and tracking it on a calendar. The jokes didn't need to be perfect. At this point, the process is more important than the results. Over time, your skill will improve, and the quality and quantity will take care of themselves. What is most important is consistency.

Whatever you settle on, track your consistency *daily*, *visibly*, and ideally *publicly*. Seeing your progress and consistency is a strong motivator. The threat of a skipped day in the chain can be enough to punch Snooze-man in the throat.

There are a million habit tracker apps on the market. I've tried a few, and many are helpful. At the end of the day, I went with a low-tech solution on the door of my office a la Seinfeld. It is a year-at-a-glance annual wall calendar that works with wet and dry erase markers. I entered the months and days with wet-erase and track my habits for two things—morning routine where I circle the date in red, and writing 500 words where I place an X in the box with blue. My wife and kids can see it when they come into my office, and more importantly, I see it all the time. Every day.

After setting up a new habit, it's essential to check in with yourself at regular intervals to review your progress. Seriously, schedule ten minutes on your actual calendar at any interval that works for you, and commit to these checkups consistently. Every Monday morning over coffee or every Sunday night after dinner or the first day of every month. Weekly is a simple option but use whatever works for you. Just do it.

Is the habit that moves you to that goal on auto-pilot? Fight the temptation to add something new before the first one is installed. If the first one isn't working, ask yourself why. Once the first one is up and running, maybe you add another one that supports the same goal? Or move on to the next thing on your list and add a new habit that supports the new goal's plan.

Every time you meet with yourself, use the following agenda as a guide to help keep yourself on track and aligned with your priorities. You don't even need to write anything down, so long as you answer each question thoughtfully. Download, edit and print out a copy for yourself at www.DadAthlon.com/Execution

Bonus: **Daily Habit Self-Meeting Agenda**

Date:

What is my target habit?

Is my target habit aligned with my goal?

Have I been doing it consistently? Is it baked into my bones?

If not, why?

>Not enough time? Shorten it to _____

>Wrong time of day? Move it to _____

>Distracted by something less important? Rethink your environment. Relocate it to _____

>Pushed aside by something more important? Reassess priorities. Do I need to replace this habit with a new one that is better aligned with my current priorities?

If yes…

>Am I ready to add a new goal/habit?

>Which one do I want to add?

>Is this habit alone sufficient to achieve my current goal?

>Do I need another habit that accelerates my progress toward my current goal or one that supports a different goal?

What is the next most important thing on my list?

What is the next skill/habit I need most right now?

What is the *smallest* daily action I know I can do *every day* to support this new habit?

How can I stack this easily on top of my current habit(s)?

Three Examples From my Own Life

Morning Routine

Early in 2020, I began a tiny morning routing after reading two helpful books. Many of this chapter's ideas are based on these books—*The Miracle Morning* by Hal Elrod and *Atomic Habits* by James Clear.

I won't do any deep dive book reports here, but I highly recommend each. If you're interested in picking up a copy, you can find links to both at www.DadAthlon.com/Execution.

In a nutshell, *The Miracle Morning* examines the value of a *simple* structured morning routine. *Atomic Habits* stresses the value of starting small because consistency is far more important than output.

I started with exercising for five minutes every day. Yep. Only five. When I worked out in the past, I always felt the need to do at least twenty, and more often, closer to thirty. Five minutes felt like not even worth the effort. Very unmanly. But if the kids needed something, or I was tired, or had an early call, I often didn't have time for twenty minutes or more. Plus, the cool-down and the need for a shower took even more time. So I'd end up maybe working out three times this week. Then two the following week.

But I can squeeze five minutes in any day. And I may not even need to shower after! Prioritizing consistency over output was an excuse vaccine. I was able to do something every single day for fourteen days. What's more, I ended up running for twenty to thirty minutes anyway on many of those days.

In permitting myself to let five minutes be enough, I not only felt great about my streak, but also, I often went well over the base goal. This led to feeling accomplishment and pride, making it easier to continue the habit and fuel further growth.

After that five-minute run was baked into my day, I added two minutes of quiet breathing. Some days I'd use a short YouTube video to keep me in the zone. Starting a few weeks after that, while I was cooling down, I'd write at least one thing I'm grateful for. Then a super scaled-back plan for the day, as in *one thing* that I absolutely committed to doing.

I ended up with a morning routine I did every single day, and in its most scaled-back fashion, I could knock out every element in ten minutes. But if I did have more time, I could expand one area or another.

I was accustomed to thinking every solution needed to be this big giant thing—that any morning routine worth doing at all would need to be at least ninety minutes. But here's the thing. Ten minutes of something *you actually do every day* beats ninety minutes of something you do sporadically for three weeks, then flame out.

Lose Weight

Once I installed my simple morning routine, I decided I needed to drop a few pounds. Technically, I *decided* I needed to lose weight way earlier, but it was only now that I decided to *do* anything about it. After doing a little research, I added intermittent fasting. I used the Zero app, which let me start slow and track my progress and consistency. It is free, easy, and intuitive.

After adjusting for a few weeks, I added another free app to help easily track calories—My Fitness Pal. I entered my goal, and it calculated my calories for me. It even offset my calories for any exercise I did in the morning, all of which created a positive feedback loop.

Because I added these habits one at a time, they built on each other naturally and organically. They weren't a shock to my system or routine and created positive results that reinforced using all of them. Eventually, I dropped thirty pounds and felt great! I barely noticed the extra effort.

Writing This Book

At the risk of breaking the fourth wall, my process of writing this book embodied exactly what I'm talking about. I started by taking full days to focus on writing *all* day. While that did help move the ball forward, it had two side effects:

1) My writing quality was not consistent over the long day. I then needed to spend more time fixing things I wrote in the latter hours of each binge session when I was getting tired.
2) I'd then feel entitled to take a day or three off. Heck, I produced so much content on my binge days I deserved it, right? The problem was I had a hard time picking up from where I left off several days earlier.

After I committed to writing fewer words each session, but consistently every day, the flow and clarity of my writing became stronger. It was also much easier to maintain over a longer timeframe.

Takeaway: Small habits built over time are far more powerful than giant buckets of effort in spurts. Start small—with the smallest unit of commitment you'll do *every day*—then build.

Pulling It All Together—The Can't-Miss, Easy 10-Step Action Plan

We've touched on a lot here, but now it's time for an action plan. The plan below is common sense and built on what we've discussed. What makes this plan tricky is not what you *do* but what you *don't* do. Saying no to everything other than your current priority is much easier said than done. Effort that is laser-focused on building *one* goal-aligned habit at a time before adding the next one will pay dividends in time. This is the secret sauce.

1) Brainstorm goal ideas. These might be related to relationships, financial goals, or health and fulfillment— uncoincidentally these map to the three sections of this book.
2) Pick *one* to focus on first. You will get to the others—limit yourself to one for now. What dad muscle group do you want to strengthen first?
3) Clarify your goal with a clear outcome—dollars, pounds, frequency. Include a specific end date—ideally less than three months. Break any longer-term goals down to something achievable in three to six months, tops.
4) Identify and *commit* to a single small daily habit that aligns with your goal and you will stick to. Every. Single. Day. When in doubt about the size of the commitment, round down. For example, the macho part of your brain will want to level up, even within small commitments. If you're wondering whether you should commit to running for five minutes or ten, pick five.
5) Share your goal/habit with someone who will help you remain accountable. Wife, buddies, online accountability partner, or bet money on yourself.
6) Do it every day until it's baked into your bones.

7) Schedule a regular ten-minute block of time on your actual calendar, and use this time to review your progress. Pick an interval that will work for you. Weekly works best for most guys. Walk through the Daily Habit Self-Meeting Agenda above to clarify and reflect on your progress.
8) Only after habit #1 is baked and on auto-pilot, determine a *single* new habit or goal to become your #2.
9) Focus *only* on habit #2 until it is likewise baked, reviewing your progress regularly.
10) Rinse. Repeat.

Summary

Fatherhood has a lot of moving parts. It is easy to simply *react* to everything the world and our kids throw at us. But if we don't decide what *we* want from our life and for our kids, there is little chance we will like the outcome.

As fathers, we need to decide *proactively* what goals are most critical, set clear plans around those, and build the habits that ensure success. Goal and plans fuel sticky habits that ensure success. While this process is not difficult, it is often neglected.

Sometimes a father tries to do too many things at once, diluting his efforts, sapping his energy, and delaying success.

Focusing on clear, small, and consistent habits one at a time is the key to building a life for you and your kids that aligns with what you value most.

Do

- Sit down and get clear about what you want most.
- Pick the one area you want to strengthen first and create a simple plan that moves you in that direction.
- *Focus* on building that habit.
- Track your habits daily and visibly.
- Check-in with yourself regularly to assess if the habit is installed or the goal is achieved.

Don't

- Try to accomplish it all at once.
- Try to install two habits at once.
- Assume a habit, once installed, will stay forever without a reason.

CHAPTER 6

DOLLARS - DEFENSE

> That is the thankless position of the father in the family—the provider for all, and the enemy of all.
>
> – J. August Strindberg

In early 2020, as it was becoming clear that COVID was here for the long haul, my wife Erin and I looked for non-device-based activities to make the most of our downtime. You can only watch so many damn movies.

Erin had a great idea. Each of the six of us would put together a five-minute presentation for the rest of the family on any topic of his or her choosing—the funnier and cleverer, the better.

The kids groaned—they're kids, it's their job—but they did it anyway. Erin and I were nervous the project would backfire, and they'd hate every minute. We were both pleasantly surprised at the creativity all four kids showed!

We had great presentations on various topics, such as:

> *Ron Swanson's Pyramid of Greatness* (from the TV show *Parks and Recreation*)
>
> *Why Shaggy* (from *Scooby-Doo*) *is a God*
>
> *Ranking our Family – Dance Mom Pyramid Style*
>
> *Why I Procrastinated Doing This Family Presentation*

If you were assigned this presentation to give to your family, what would *your* topic be?

Personally, I didn't have to think very hard. My topic was:

> *Shedding Light On…Light: The Top Ten Lights Most Frequently Left On*

Can I get an Amen?

And I know *you* know it was hard for me to *limit* myself to only ten! As in, there were many more candidates than ten to pick from.

My presentation was sublime. A tour-de-force, even. It included powerful and memorable slides such as:

1) Thoughtful and profound quotes about light by Maya Angelou, Victor Hugo, and even Jesus. Following these quotes was a question. What do these light experts have in common?

    Answer: *None* of them is paying our electric bill.

2) What happens when you leave the light on?

   Answer: Puppies cry, complete with pictures of crying puppies.

3) Pandemics break out when you leave lights on. This slide included a meme saying, "I'm no expert on COVID-19, but this is The Cure," written over a picture of the band The Cure.

The meat of the presentation was a photo tour of the most well-illuminated yet vacant rooms of my house.

My favorite was a picture of my daughter studying at the dining room table with the lights off. Then the same scene, *moments later*—daughter is gone, and somehow, lights are *on*.

> BONUS: Interested in seeing my slides? Take a look www.DadAthlon.com/Dollars. There are only 25 slides, and it goes pretty quick. Let me know what you think.

You get me. You've been there.

Have you tried this? Bring kids into the bathroom. Turn the faucet on. Walk out. We all agree no one does *that*. Tell them it's the same thing as the lights!

Did that work for you?

Yeah, me neither.

Why the hell are we like that? My dad was a stickler about the lights too. We know. The stress of providing is hard-wired into the psyche of dad-ness. Leaving the lights on is a minor but super-visible affront to everything dads do to pay the mortgage, save for college, and bankroll vacations. Making ends meet is the most taken-for-granted activity a dad does. If there is one topic that creates the greatest stress for dad and *between* parents, it's bringing home the bacon.

In the triathlon of dad-ness, effectively managing finances often feels like the biggest key to the gold medal. The goal of the next two chapters is to develop strategies to build strength in this event. We will share ideas and exercises to ensure that, like Cheerios, your financial picture will be part of this balanced breakfast of dad-ness.

When it comes to optimizing dollars for the DadAthlon, there are two flavors.

Defense—protecting the money going out the door.

Offense—increasing the money coming in the door.

We'll talk through each of these, but a brief word before we do. This is not a book about why or how various ideas might be worthwhile—other books can walk you through the math of *why* starting early makes sense, and compound interest, and more math, and the minutiae of financial strategies. And ugh!

Yep. All that stuff is valuable and important. It's just not relevant to our present goal.

An athlete doesn't *need* to know what his amino acids are doing as he recovers between his interval training workouts.

Do amino acids exist? Yes.

Are they essential for an athlete's body? Probably.

Does he give a crap? Well, it would be interesting if he did, but almost certainly, he does not.

For the most part, we will be taking for granted the whys and mechanics *behind* these ideas and resources. Our focus will be the how, the pros and cons, and simple and effective implementation. I say that now because I know what you may be thinking when we start with…

Defense

The best offense is a good defense.

Good pitching beats good hitting.

Warren Buffet's 2 Rules of Investing:

> Rule #1 - Don't lose money.
> Rule #2 - When in doubt, see Rule #1.

Two things about financial defense are noteworthy:

First, it's low-hanging fruit. If your boss offered you a *permanent* $300 a month raise tomorrow to come in on a Saturday morning for four hours to clean up the office, would you take the deal? Of course, you would! Spoiler alert: You're about to make yourself the same offer.

Second, strong defense *enables* better offense. In football, a strong defense creates a better starting field position for the offense. The less money you waste, the more you have to spend on the things you decide are most important for your family.

I've found financial defense requires two basic skill sets—hiding and budgeting (Ouch! You knew I'd say it eventually, but stick with me).

Much ink has been spilled on budgeting, and I will not add much to that beyond my single favorite quote about its importance.

"Budgeting is telling your money where to go instead of wondering where it went." –John C. Maxwell, author, pastor, and leadership expert.

As for hiding, the importance of this strategy to a strong defense can also be summed up in a single sentence. Protect your money from—wait for it…—*yourself*!

We'll start with budgeting, which does not need to be as annoying as you think it will be. And remember, you'd take that permanent $300 raise for four hours of office cleanup, so stick with me.

The steps are:

1) Find the leaks—review where your money goes and identify those places it shouldn't.
2) Fix all the leaks—this step is the fun one.
3) Tame the *budget-busters*—those semi-unexpected expenses that blow up your month.
4) Manage discretionary expenses—with a well-designed and *simple budget*, you only need to manage two to four discretionary categories to be successful.

Let's walk through each step.

Find the Leaks

From time to time, you schedule half a day to do annoying stuff around the house. Maybe it's cleaning the garage or doing yard work in the fall or spring. Swap out the mower and rakes for the snowblower and shovels. Schedule the furnace cleaning. Sometimes you tackle that list of six totally unrelated things that have accumulated over the past two months to ten years—the things your wife used to remind you about sweetly, and now you just need to tackle them.

But how do you feel when you get that stuff done?

Relief? Yeah.

Accomplishment? Of course.

Proud? Probably.

An extra $300 in your pocket? Maybe not. But dang, that sure would be the cherry on top.

Rather than spend half a Saturday fixing the *actual* leaks around your house, let's use that same time to fix the financial leaks.

What follows is a proven process to fix your financial leaks quickly and easily. This will help get you on track to hit and exceed the financial goals you have prioritized for your family.

The quickest way to find all the leaky pipes in your house is to remove all the walls. Hard to do in a house. Very simple with your dollars. Easily accomplished on paper.

If you prefer a computer over paper or if you have accounts at several banks, you can also do the same thing electronically using free software. Financial aggregators like Mint combine your financial data into a single snapshot. Refer to the following Dad Hack for more details.

> Dad Hack: One resource that makes viewing all your accounts and transactions easy is a financial aggregator. After setting it up with the login details from all your accounts, these sites provide a thorough picture of your *entire* financial health. This makes the process of finding leaks a one-stop shop. You can see reports like what categories you spend the most on and your net worth over time.
>
> Some banks and financial advisors themselves offer versions of this service, so check with yours.
>
> Or you can sign up for a free account at Mint—which will connect your accounts and help you track most expenses. www.mint.com
>
> Personal Capital has useful free tools. It provides more robust reporting and planning for a fee if you're interested in deeper analysis or guidance. www.personalcapital.com
>
> Each serves a slightly different purpose, and as such, each has its pros and cons depending on your needs.

The review process is the same, although electronically, you can save time by sorting or filtering certain payees or categories. If the aggregator you select is particularly smart, it might "smell" the category of an expense based on the payee and show you a report or a graph. They are usually good about categorizing things like groceries or gas but may need a little input from you if Amazon or Target shows up a lot.

For *now*, don't worry about making sure the categories are correct on those squishy ones. We are looking for transactions that are clear and jump off the page as candidates for a cleanup.

In a nutshell, here's the process.

1) Print out the last twelve statements from your bank. Or log in to an aggregator site that will combine the last twelve months of transactions online. Get the highlighter out and highlight everything that is not absolutely essential.
2) Look for transactions that *easily* fit into one of the following three buckets.

    Eliminate
    Reduce
    Plan For

    We'll discuss each in detail below. You might consider using different color highlighters for each category, like pink, yellow, and green respectively, or creating tags if using Mint.

3) Take action to fix the leaks.

You might be asking, "Why twelve months and not only one or two?" Two reasons.

First, some of the biggest or sneakiest leaks you will find will not be from the last few months. Remember that online membership for the home workouts you signed up for two years ago? Curse you, Tony Horton!

Or the electronic newsletter from three years ago you no longer read? You know how many such memberships tell you how much you save if you get billed annually instead of monthly? Exactly! Annual billing is easier to forget about. If you see the same charge showing up every month, it's more visible and creates eleven more opportunities for you to remember to cancel it. But those *annual* payments come and go, and you may never notice them.

Second, you may also have expenses you *do* want or need that occur irregularly throughout the year, possibly only once or twice. You need to know what those are and how much they are if you're going to reduce them or plan for them.

You will likely be shell-shocked at how much you spend on coffee, movies, or Amazon over the course of a year—I'm guilty on all counts. If you want to have some fun with this, guess how much it will be for certain categories; do it with your wife if you're particularly brave or foolish and want to see what bad guessers you are.

Let's dive further into each of these three buckets.

Eliminate

These are expenses that you may have needed or wanted a while back but are no longer a priority. Some of these will be easy to toss. Others will pull at your soul with sweet temptations like, "I know we haven't been to Costco in two years, but if we ever *do* go again, we'll save a ton of money." Screw that. You can always add back the things that do make sense later. But for *this* round, jump balls go to the knife. Some examples might be old gym memberships, online subscriptions you don't use, bank fees that can be renegotiated.

Reduce

This category speaks for itself. These are expenses you do need to spend *something* on but really ought to be spending less. Below are some examples of areas where you can reduce.

Television or Streaming Services

Do you guys *really* watch HULU, Netflix, HBO, Disney+, Amazon Prime, *and* need all the channels on your cable? If you're like us, probably not. My guess is 95% of what you watch is on your top three or fewer. What you would potentially miss will likely be available soon on one of the others anyway. Consider, it doesn't matter *when* you hit every show on your list, as long as you do eventually.

Cable, Internet, Wireless: Some examples beyond TV include wireless carriers. Cable, internet, and wireless providers always offer various packages. Give them a call, tell them you're thinking about switching and have them give you their best options.

Treats

We spent way more on Dunkin' coffee than I care to admit publicly. When it comes to some treats, reducing may not mean less but where and how. Dunkin' coffee is close to my heart. When I decided to dial back, I planned to budget a defined automatic transfer to my Dunkin' App and *no more*.

But since I knew that would be hard, to offset that a bit, I let myself buy more Dunkin' K-cups. I keep the coffee cups I do get from Dunkin' when I order there. Then when I make my K-cup coffees at home, I drink them from the reused Dunkin cups. Just to be clear, while I love the Earth as much as the next guy, I am *not* doing this for the environment. And yes, I know this is odd in a semi-neurotic sort of way.

But for me, this unusual small step allows me to trick my brain into thinking I'm having real Dunkin' coffee. This is just unbullshit enough to keep me from continuously topping off the funds in my Dunkin' app. Get creative. Trick yourself if you need to—as long as it works.

Credit card debt

If you have more than one credit card, consolidating might help out with two issues.

Consolidation helps you save on interest since most card consolidation offers have a much lower promotional rate than all your existing cards. Be sure to read the fine print since the rate may be 0% for ten months, but there is a fee of 4% of the transfer. It may *still* make sense; just do the math.

The other budget advantage is that you now have one bill to pay instead of two or more with their cumulative minimums. Obviously, paying off credit card debt as soon as possible should always be plan A. When that is not immediately doable, getting smart about *how* you pay off debt is the next best thing.

ReFi

Mortgage payments are often the largest household monthly expense. Although they are not quite as simple to change as others we've discussed, it can be worth the effort to look into refinancing. As we go to press, rates remain near historic lows. A new rate that is only a little lower can save several hundred dollars a month right off the bat. There are many easy places to look online. Most options are relatively cheap, easy, and fast, with lots of feedback available on good lenders. Just be sure to do the math on the cost versus the savings. Check out www.Bankrate.com for rates on all kinds of products from a wide variety of lenders. It also has a helpful calculator for you to do the math on whether it makes sense for you. https://www.bankrate.com/mortgages/refinance-rates

> Dad Hack: ReFi + Consolidate. With interest rates so low, refinancing a mortgage will reduce your monthly payment. But if you have adequate equity in your home, you may also be able to take out some extra cash to pay off other debt, like credit cards or car loans. The rate will be a little higher than if you do not take cash out, but this may be worthwhile if it still lowers your rate and you can extinguish some other debt. That lowers both your monthly expenses and the total amount of interest you would pay your creditors over time. Only one big giant fat catch: *don't* run up the balance again on your credit card. Consider cutting up the cards, and don't go out and buy another car! For additional resources and information on ReFi, visit www.DadAthlon.com/Dollars

Accountant

If you do your own taxes, it may be worthwhile to meet with an accountant. Tax software is generally pretty good, and a good accountant is not cheap. But discussing your specific situation as well as your recent returns with a human expert may be worth the investment. COVID ushered in more working from home, new tax laws, and several versions of stimulus. If cleaning out your garage over half a Saturday is worth a modest permanent raise, spending a few hundred dollars to keep hundreds more in your pocket is also worth considering.

Plan For

This third bucket of expenses include things that are mission-critical to your family but may annoy the crap out of you when they show up. Examples include fees for kids' activities, birthday parties, car tax. You *know* these items are out there. But that still doesn't keep you from being pissed when they arrive. And worst of all, they blow up your monthly budget just as fast as something totally unexpected. For now, let's simply identify what these things are as you go through the last year. Another name for these types of expenses is "variable with benefits." Further below, we'll explain that term and discuss a proven strategy for ensuring these never blow up your budget again.

Fix the Leaks

At this point we've reviewed the last twelve months and *found* the leaks, categorizing various transactions into the buckets of eliminate, reduce or plan for. Now it's time to take *action* and *fix* the leaks.

Let's begin with steps and actions that target the "eliminate" and "reduce" buckets. We'll discuss "plan for" in the next section.

None of these ideas is as difficult as you might fear. Don't let the fear of it being a big hassle prevent you from doing anything. Just come up with your list. You've already set aside your metaphorical Saturday morning. You have the playbook. Now all you need to do is run the plays.

Here are some sample action steps to fix these leaks.

Quick & Easy

- Cancel memberships including unused gym/fitness, wholesale clubs, subscriptions of any kind—sorry, jelly of the month club!
- Renegotiate with
    - Cable
    - Phone
    - Internet
- Thin out redundant extra streaming services.
- Replace some treats with less expensive substitutions.

Bigger Picture

- Consolidate credit cards.
- ReFi house/car.
- Call an accountant to assess tax opportunities.

Why Budgeting Sucks!

Before we can effectively tame the budget busters, it's useful to spend some time on how and why budgets often *don't* work. You may not have expected to see a "Budgeting Sucks" heading *right* when we are about to get into more depth about budgeting. But it's critical that an effective budgeting strategy fix or mitigate the following pain points.

"Budgets are a lot of work to set up and manage."

"I hate tediously tracking every expense."

"My wife and I aren't on the same page."

"It's easy on paper but hard in the real world."

"I don't want to deprive myself/kids/family of anything."

"It's impossible to plan for those surprise expenses and still stay on track."

"I can budget all my fixed expenses easily but struggle with those that are variable or discretionary."

All of which add up to a big fat, "What's the point?!"

Any of those sound familiar? They do to me. In fairness, I did just write them. But I have thought versions of all those comments many times—loudly and often—enough to have me just give up on this budgeting racket altogether! Until, of course, I find myself *once again* writing "pay off credit cards" on my list of goals for the year. Didn't I *do* that already? In 2018? And also in 2015? What the hell?

You get the idea. We know budgeting is important. And that it works. But those pain points are real. What can we do to reduce or remove those obstacles enough to want to budget well?

As dads, we are accustomed to teaching our kids about the value of doing things that are hard but worth it. Well, karma's a bitch. But the good news is *your* kids won't need to know how easy we can make this.

To address the pain points, our approach to budgeting is designed to be simple, automatic, life-proof, and effective. It is grounded in three principles.

1) Fixed Autopilot: Make as many expenses as possible work within a fixed monthly amount. The magic lies in

transforming choppy and unpredictable ones into a fixed amount.
2) Few Variables: Tracking three things is way easier than tracking ten. Who knew? The fewer variables to manage, the easier it is and the higher likelihood of success.
3) Easy and Fail-Safe: Make good decisions be the path of least resistance. Going over budget is doable, but only with eyes wide open and when you choose to do so.

Now that we have fixed all the minor leaks above, the next step is to protect yourself from budget-busters. For the purposes of this metaphor, these are life's burst pipes.

You've been there. You did your budget. You're being good. You only bought three coffees last week. Then it happens—the car needs a new radiator; you forgot about the fee for junior's baseball team; your twins get invited to a bar mitzvah which itself is *for twins*. Yes, that invitation really happened.

Then two things occur.

First, your budget is blown up! After all that damn work, you're upside down on your well-constructed plan.

Second, and most importantly and dangerously, you say, "Screw it!" After throwing your hands in the air, you just buy the damn pitching wedge or surround sound system anyway. You're already in the hole now, so if you're going to have a credit card balance anyway, you might as well enjoy it! Yep. Been there. Well, for the pitching wedge anyway.

But here's the thing. In our house, *most* of the items that blew up our budget happened regularly, just not in clear monthly or bi-weekly intervals. It turns out our budget got blown up *every* March by baseball. And every September by birthdays and every December by Christmas. If only there were a way to predict these expenses and plan for them…

These are the "variable with benefits" expenses. They are variable in the sense that they are not the same from month to month. But the *benefit* is that they are predictable on an annual basis. We can plan for them and, in so doing, transform them *into* fixed expenses. These are the plan for expenses we identified above. Variable with benefits is a bit cumbersome to say—and write! So we'll abbreviate these as VarB's. Some of the things that fall into this category for us are:

Gifts: Birthdays, Christmas and all the gifts for our kids' friends. Many sneak up on us.

Car Repair: This doesn't have the regular cadence of other expenses. But between the variability of time and cost, car repair was a big offender. Car tax often falls into this category.

Heating Oil: Great in the summer; in the winter, not so much.

Irregular Home Maintenance: Clean the furnace, pump the septic, close the pool.

Kids' Activities: Dance, soccer, karate, school trip.

The Stupid Dog: He's mostly on autopilot from an expense mode. Then you take him to the vet, and he has diphtheria, gout, and early onset dog-mentia, all of which require a stool sample— there's no *not* doing that—as well as specialized medicine and prescription dog food.

Emergency/Rainy Day/Miscellaneous: In *The Total Money Makeover*, financial guru Dave Ramsey talks about Murphy. Unless you

Murphy-proof your life, he will show up. I don't know about you, but that has been our experience. This is a catch-all for what life *will* throw at you someday.

Upon first review, reining in our spending felt a lot like herding cats. But as we reviewed the types and timing of our expenses, they all fell into one of three clear categories: fixed, variable with benefits (VarB's), and *truly* variable, which we'll call discretionary.

Fixed Expenses

These expenses are basically the same dollar amounts every month. These include mortgage and car payments, insurance, TV, phone, some utilities, debt, savings, and charity. These expenses are rarely the reasons people wring their hands about budgeting. They are already *on* auto-pilot. You barely need to look at them, much less touch them.

Variable With Benefits / VarB's

The benefits here refer to the fact that these expenses can *become* fixed. These payments are not necessarily the same each month but are mostly predictable over the course of a year. Once we do the math, we can set aside a *fixed* amount each month for these variable expenses. These are also the rat bastards that sneak up on us and blow up our budgets. Some examples are car repairs/taxes, kids' activity fees, home maintenance, birthday and holiday gifts.

Discretionary

Discretionary encompasses everything else. The million little things where most of the budget abuse happens—coffee, lunch out, movie, coffee again, candy while picking up that prescription, car scraper from Amazon, toilet repair kit from Home Depot, drinks after work, another coffee. This is also where budget tracking apps feel particularly tedious when you're Venmoing $1.09 to Iron Balls McGinty. For coffee.

Now that we're clear on the types of expenses, what do we *do* with that information?

The object of the game is simple:

Minimize the number of Discretionary expenses by moving as many expenses as possible from Discretionary to VarB's.

Then you can provide for *both* Fixed and VarB's using using fixed monthly amounts, which you set up on auto-pilot.

By converting these expenses to auto-pilot, the process is easier because there are no actions to take. It is also much simpler since it reduces the number of remaining discretionary expenses to manage. This process will be your shield against budget-busters *and is* the key to staying within your budget.

Because these VarB expenses are predictable in the long run, automatically saving for them each month transforms them from variable to fixed.

Now all you have left are expenses that are truly squishy or discretionary but which you need help controlling.

"But Tim, that all sounds great. On paper. But I've done this before, and my wife and I share an account. It's hard for us to know or manage how much money in our account(s) is actually earmarked for gifts or car tax, or baseball, much less how much we've spent on groceries already this month. Or to know that maybe today isn't the best day to stock up on New York strips and Ho'Ho's. What I need is something to hide this money from myself *until* I need it. I also need something *easy* to keep both my wife and me within our budget for the expenses we have every week."

Great idea. Glad you thought of it. Two goals here:

Goal 1: Tame budget-busters / VarB's.

Tool: Use escrow accounts to stay ahead of VarB expenses.

Goal 2: Manage your simple budget by focusing on your two to four truly variable expense categories.

Tool: Prepaid debit cards for discretionary expenses that vary.

Tame the Budget Busters

Escrow accounts and prepaid debit cards are effective tools that rely on the same strategy—protect yourself from *yourself*. The plan is to hide dollars so they don't accidentally get spent, but you know exactly where they are when you need them.

The first tool is to use escrow accounts for VarB's. This is for large, less frequent, but predictable expenses. Examples include car repair and kids' activities. The idea is to protect money from yourself in a way that also funds *for* these unexpected expenses. This technique allows you to trick yourself into sticking to a budget by using a bunch of little pre-defined rainy-day funds.

Best Practice: Make it easy to transfer into and out of these accounts, but not *too* easy. You want it to be liquid with no transaction fees, so no CDs or mutual funds. Ideally, not in the same bank as your everyday accounts, since the temptation to transfer immediately can be very seductive. We use Capital One 360 for all our escrow accounts. We have several accounts in there, and it takes three days for the transfer to get to our checking account or credit card. This is enough of a waiting period to ensure we don't get *too* impulsive.

Steps to setting up and using your escrow accounts:

1) Determine *your* VarB categories (your "plan for" bucket from earlier.)
2) Figure out how much you've spent in each category over the last year.
3) Divide by twelve.
4) Add 5-10% as a margin for safety.
5) Include that amount as your initial budget item—now newly baptized as a fixed monthly expense. Each month transfer that amount into an escrow account you've set up in each VarB category.
6) As those expenses arise, you transfer the funds from your escrow bucket back to your checking account or credit card to pay for it in full. No budgets or animals are harmed in the process.

> Dad Hack: Easy to use escrow account: For years, we have used Capital One 360. You can set up accounts in five minutes for free. Funding and transfers are easy and free. They are a reputable bank and pay higher than average interest rates on savings accounts, which is what we use for our escrows. You can have a ton of accounts if you decide you have many categories you want to pre-fund. The only semi-downside is that transfers to and from external accounts take two to three days. If you are using the accounts as suggested above, that isn't a problem since you wouldn't need large amounts of cash immediately. We've had accounts there since 2001, and they work very well for this purpose.
>
> Bonus: Capital One 360 also has great accounts for kids and teens, which you can link easily to your adult accounts. This encourages your kids to save and spend wisely. It also enables oversight and easy, immediate transfers for mowing the lawn or going to the movies.

Try to recategorize as many expenses as possible from discretionary to VarB so that you can fund them through your escrow accounts. The goal is to be able to achieve your monthly budget by controlling as few variables as possible.

In our case, we found that there were only three types of *truly* variable expenses that required our attention to prevent overspending. These are groceries, gas, and flex/cash, which we used as a catch-all for uncategorized or unpredictable small expenses like the gum and the coffees and the ice scraper and the girl scout cookies. To make our entire budget of *all* of our expenses work well, those are the only three things we need to focus on.

Once you're down to three things to focus on, then what? We found we spent more on groceries than seemed reasonable. The biggest culprit was that, while we knew we had a budget for groceries and even knew the dollar amount, we often didn't know how much we had already spent.

Many phone apps are available to help you keep track, and that is certainly one approach. But it often takes an extra step to enter or categorize every single expense every single time, and for these apps to work, you and your wife need to consistently follow through. Not impossible, but for me, if I have two options for fixing a problem, I prefer the one that tends to be simpler and more foolproof.

Manage Discretionary Expenses

Enter our second tool—the shared pre-paid debit card. It helps us manage the accumulation of unplanned or variable expenses that occur throughout the month. This strategy prevents us from spending more than we intend without full consent of the will. We can go over if needed, but only if we transfer from someplace else.

Use the following four steps to employ this approach.

1) Determine what categories of expenses you need to manage regularly. For us, they are groceries, flex/cash, and gas.
2) Figure out how much you spent last year in each bucket. Then, in the context of your present needs, determine how much you ought to spend for each this year.
3) Transfer those amounts monthly onto pre-funded debit cards. This operates as an electronic version of the envelope system made popular by Dave Ramsey's *The Total Money Makeover*. We use the Akimbo Card.

We direct deposit part of our paychecks onto a prepaid debit card. Though it is technically one prepaid debit card, it creates several sub-accounts, each with separate cards. My wife and I each have debit cards called gas and cash. We share a groceries card by each pointing Apple Pay to that card number. The Akimbo app lets you see your balance *and* transfer dollars from one to the other. FamZoo is another excellent option with similar features.

4) Repeat. The value here is twofold. First, this technique prevents tracking small expenses manually or even semi-automatically. It is automatic. Second, it is flexible. We can spend more if we *need* to. But the catch is, unlike a credit card or a no-budget approach, we *know* we are doing it. We transfer the extra from another category with our eyes wide open. For example, in the first few months of COVID, we spent a lot more on groceries, but we moved it from our gas card, where we were spending a lot less. And the best news is, *overall*, we were still within our budget, even though we were never explicitly trying to do so.

> Dad Hack: Split Direct Deposit. Many people have their paycheck directly deposited into their checking account. But what they do *not* know is that most of the time, that money can be deposited into several different accounts. This is not nearly as tricky as most people think it is. Call your HR/payroll person, and likely you'll have only a very simple half-page form to complete. Within two or three pay cycles, you can have $500 go here, $250 go there, and the rest into your normal checking account.

In a nutshell, these tools help put fixed and VarB expenses on auto-pilot. We tame the VarB's using escrow accounts and manage the few remaining discretionary expenses with pre-paid debit cards.

Summary

Great financial defense enables better financial offense. Several easy and valuable strategies to level up your defense include fixing leaks, planning for irregular but predictable expenses, hiding money from yourself, and minimizing truly variable expenses to two to three categories. This helps put most of the heavy lifting of telling your money where to go on auto-pilot.

Some tools that help accomplish these strategies are financial aggregators, escrow accounts, and pre-paid debit cards.

Like cleaning up the office on a Saturday in exchange for a *permanent* raise, these strategies and tools require some effort on the front end, but once implemented, run on auto-pilot and pay dividends for years to come.

Do

- ➢ Find the leaks—review twelve months of transactions to determine where your money is going.
- ➢ Fix the leaks—categorize the leaks into one of the following fixes:
    - o Eliminate
    - o Reduce/Renegotiate
    - o Plan For/Variable with Benefits

- Create a simple budget where every type of expense is one of the following:
    - Fixed/AutoPilot
    - Variable with Benefits
    - Discretionary
- Set up escrow accounts for all Plan For/VarB items so that you can budget for them as a Fixed/Autopilot item. This leads to budget-buster immunity.
- Set up prepaid debit cards for the 2-4 expense types that fall under Discretionary. The fewer, the better.
- Modify your direct deposits so that the appropriate amounts are automatically whisked away into these pre-planned buckets.

Don't

- Wait.
- Skimp on the number of months you analyze.

CHAPTER 7

DOLLARS - OFFENSE

> Money is not the goal. Money has no value. The value comes from the dreams money helps achieve.
>
> – Robert Kiyosaki

I don't know if you've heard, but it turns out college can be rather expensive these days. This message is so pervasively drummed into parents from day-one that pregnancy test kits should include 529 plan brochures!

We began saving *some* money for college *sort of* early in our parenting journey. As the number of kids in our house increased, our contributions did not keep pace. Then one day, I decided to get more clarity on exactly how much money for college I should be saving.

I like spreadsheets, so I built an awesome one for college savings. I'll spare you the details—if you're curious, check it out www.DadAthlon.com/Dollars. I enter average tuition and an average rate of inflation. The tool then does all the calculations and returns how much money we would need to save for each kid and by what date. It also showed a grand total—the full cost of putting four kids through reasonable colleges.

When I saw that number, I thought, "Surely one of my formulas must be wrong! I mean, I know it will be a lot, but holy crap!" After scouring all my formulas, the good news was that my formulas were correct. The bad news was an eye-popping number that seemed ridiculously out of reach.

Effective college planning strategies use various investments, experts, testing resources, loans, scholarships, and schools. And that is just the start. Cataloging and discussing these resources is beyond the scope of this book. At the end of the day, the rubber hits the road with actual dollars tucked away into whichever plan(s) you select. The savviest strategy in the world means jack squat if you don't have enough nickels set aside to make it work.

This is where a strong financial *offense* began for me. Our strong defense has fixed all the leaks in our budget, protected us from budget-busters, and created more dollars at the end of the month. Now we turn our attention to bringing more dollars in through the front door.

Your Why

Before we dig into the nitty-gritty of better financial offense, let's take a moment to talk about your *why*. Having more dollars is generally better than having fewer. Everyone understands that. But for what purpose?

Many men understand what motivates them to succeed, including non-fathers. But dads have a louder motivating *why* behind most of what they do, and the answer is often their kids. The birth of his first child shifts how a man perceives his purpose in the world, at least compared to before. And that is as it should be.

As we strive to improve our financial offense, it's important to get clearer on *exactly why*. A man can spend seventy hours a week on the job, earning as much money as he possibly can, telling himself it is "for the kids." What's more, he may believe that. But *how* is it for the kids, specifically?

Earning money for the kids so we have money for the kids is like a football coach saying, "I want to build a strong offense so that we can have the best offense in the league." The *purpose* of a good offense is to score points to win the game. Get clear on what game you're playing. Is it college? Annual vacations? Debt? Figure it out. Add it up. Write it down. Then plan your strategy so that you achieve those goals. Then you also can allocate enough time and attention to the other dad muscle groups.

Like a triathlon, the DadAthlon is about *balanced* strength. An Iron Man triathlon entails a 2.4-mile swim, a 112-mile bike ride, and a 26.2-mile run. In the race, it would be silly for someone to swim four miles because they can. And it would be worse if it's because they are unclear on how much swimming the race requires. All that extra swimming takes precious time and energy away from their bike and run, jeopardizing their ability to finish the race at all.

Similarly, when planning your financial offense playbook, figure out how far you need to swim to hit your goals. Then get out of the water and get on your bike. Don't swim any farther than necessary to finish the race. Especially when all your bike really wants is to play catch in the yard.

> Dad Hack: Financial Offense Goal Planner. Take ten minutes and write down what specific goals you have for your kids and family that are tied to dollar amounts. Think about how much you need and when. Compare that to how much you have and will continue to earn. Will you have enough, or is there a gap? How big is the gap? *That* is your financial offense goal you should work toward as you plan your offense.

One-And-Done

Financial offense comes in two flavors, one-and-done and cash flow.

One-and-Done: As the name suggests, these strategies bring money into the house in a non-repetitive manner. The best and easiest example is selling property you own.

Cash Flow: These strategies produce a continuous flow of income.

Which ones you consider depends on your goals and the time you can allocate. In some cases, your expertise and ability to learn new skills are also important factors.

If your defense is solid, and all you want to do is achieve a specific goal like pay off a little debt or save for a vacation, a one-and-done approach might be fine. The secret side benefit of selling stuff you already own is the additional peace of mind you get by also having less clutter.

Below are eleven great one-and-done ideas for making money selling your stuff.

Your Home Itself

Alright, we'll start with the big one. This is obviously a big step, but also the one with the highest potential return. How much depends on your debt, your market, your goals, and your living requirements. If you're reading this book, it's unlikely you're an empty nester, so downsizing may not be easy. But if you do have some unused space, your real estate market has heated up lately and you now work from home, or you plan to relocate in the medium term anyway, it may be worth a look. You can sell now and cash in, then downsize or rent for a bit. If any of the above scenarios are something other than a clear no, it's worth calling a capable agent to get a sense of your local market and options.

Furniture

We're talking about *extra* furniture you no longer need since selling a couch for $200 to replace it with a $2,000 couch defeats the purpose. But furniture is very expensive, which means there is a nice market out there for stuff that is in decent shape. Because furniture is hard to sell outside your local area, Craigslist is a great place to list a few things and see what you can get. If your stuff isn't *quite* pristine, and you live near a college, consider posting flyers on campus, especially if it's August or, to a lesser extent, December or January. Social media is another great option. Offer a discount if they pick it up themselves.

Your Car

Like furniture, the idea here is to walk away with more dollars in your pocket. Thus, this assumes you will either not replace your car or replace it with something less expensive. Pocket the difference, win the game. This only works if you own and do not lease your car and works *best* if you own it outright with no remaining payments. This might be a good strategy if mom drives the nicer, larger family car and you only need yours to get back and forth to work. If dollars are worth more than a few creature comforts and the math works out, trade down.

Here's one example: Sell the four-year-old SUV you bought new for $45,000 on a six-year loan. If it's currently worth $25,000, pay off the remaining $10,000 balance, and have $15,000 left to buy a reliable eight- to ten-year-old Camry with 80,000 miles for $12,000. You now have $3,000 in your pocket *and no car payment.*

Where to sell it: You can list it on Craiglist to maximize what you can get for it. If you go this route, prepare for lots of meetings and calls from folks who aren't really interested. Others may only low-ball you after wasting your time taking your car to *their* mechanic. With patience, though, this can pay off. Carmax is another good alternative for a sure thing, but you will trade dollars for hassle. If that is a trade you can live with, they are a great option and make the process very easy.

DVDs/CDs

With everything streaming these days, this isn't exactly a growth market. Still, plenty of folks are out there with DVD and CD players looking to add to their collection. Light and cheap to ship, these may be worth the effort, but probably not a large bang for your buck one at a time. Depending on the title and condition, used DVDs are likely to fetch between fifty cents to a few dollars each. But hey, every nickel counts. One thought is to bundle them into packages like potato chip variety packs. *Four Weddings and a Funeral* might just be the BBQ potato chip of your DVD bundle. If you want top dollar, consider eBay for direct selling. If you're willing to take less money to save time and aggravation of ads, questions, and negotiating, consider Decluttr. They buy used DVDs, CDs, books, electronics, toys, and more in a no-fuss, no-muss manner. Check them out at https://www.decluttr.com/how-it-works/.

Books

Books are like DVDs above on all counts, including using Declutter for sales. Amazon is also a possible place to list used books, although the setup to sell stuff on Amazon is a little more rigorous than eBay or Decluttr. Another option is your old college textbooks, presumably in a subject that doesn't change much with time. These usually fetch more per book than your old John Grisham's will. Three options to consider are:

> https://bookscouter.com/
> https://www.sellbackyourbook.com/
> https://www.bookfinder.com/buyback/

Old Laptops, Computers, and Phones

While *you* may be done with your old laptops, plenty of folks are eager to trade RAM and speed for dollars to meet their basic needs. Consider eBay and Decluttr, but also posting at colleges, highs schools, and libraries. Warning: Before you sell or give your computers to anyone, be 100% sure you have backed up/saved everything you need *and* wiped it completely clean. The specific process will vary, but Googling "how to completely erase my [your model computer] before selling it" will point you in the right direction.

Sports Equipment

I don't know about you, but my kids keep selfishly growing. Depending on what sports your kids used to play, this is another category where you can pad your bank account. Equipment is expensive new, but far cheaper gently used. Parents, like us, may be iffy on spending top dollar if their kid will outgrow the gear in six months. Skates, hockey gear, skis, and snowboards are all good candidates. So are golf clubs, catcher's gear, and other baseball or softball equipment like bats and gloves. In addition, the nice bags your kids used to haul around all their stuff might also be good to sell. Play It Again Sports is a good place to start locally. If you want to sell online, try eBay. Another good online option is Sideline Swap, which is an online marketplace specifically for sports equipment.

Bikes

Semi-related to sports equipment are old bikes. Take the bike down to the local bike shop. They may buy it from you or know someone who wants it. Alternatively, post flyers in coffee shops in town, add it to a neighbor's tag sale, or list it on Craigslist.

Toys and Video Game Consoles

Like everything, these should be in decent condition to be sold, and how much you get will vary based on what it is and its condition. But there are plenty of people out there looking for these. Try eBay as a good place to try to get top dollar, especially if you're selling closer to the holidays. Decluttr will also take these off your hands with less hassle but for less money.

Tools

Oh, yeah, there's that drill you got in a grab bag three years ago, but you already *had* a drill. What about that rachet set your dad gave you when you went to college. You know which tools you use and which you don't, and which ones where you are a little unsure what the hell they even *do*. Do you feel weirdly guilty every time you go to your tool area for a hammer to hang a picture? Do you see the still unopened Dremel, which you *thought* you would use twice a week? Enough is enough—to Craigslist, eBay, or Facebook Marketplace they go!

Jewelry

It's great to sell, assuming your stuff has no sentimental value. This isn't one I'd recommend selling online. But if you have half a day, walk your stuff around to a few local jewelers and get their thoughts and quotes. Obviously, what you get depends on what you got, but prepare yourself for the fact that your offers may be on the lower end of what you imagine. Still, if you're in the "something is better than nothing" camp and have a lot of stuff, this could be worth the time. The American Gem Society has some nice tips on their website, which you can link to from www.DadAthlon.com/Dollars. You can also search for a credentialed jeweler near you on their website.

Places You Can Sell Your Stuff

We discussed a few marketplaces above. Below is a little more detail on each.

eBay: The best option for trying to get the most bang for your buck with not a large amount of effort. They will take a fee, and no sales are guaranteed, but flexible and worth the effort.

Declutter: The best option for those who care more about avoiding hassle than getting top dollar. Good reputation and fast payments.

Craiglist: Great for selling things locally, especially those that are more expensive or difficult to ship, like furniture and equipment.

Amazon: *Huge* breadth, but a little more complex to set up and get up and running if you only plan to sell a few items.

Facebook Marketplace: Take advantage of your network of contacts creating some warm leads or giving you the heads up.

Garage/tag/yard sales: You can go old school and just sell your stuff straight to passersby from the front yard. These can be a lot of work to organize, so you might consider going in with a few neighbors for a bigger event. Or, some larger sales are sponsored by local municipalities or organizations. Like with anything, there is a trade-off between effort—of doing it yourself versus a town-wide event—and dollars you'll bring in. You decide what works best for you.

Finally, you may have stuff that doesn't fit neatly into any of the above categories. When in doubt, Google "best place online to sell [your specific item]" and see what comes up. You may be surprised at how many options you have.

Cash Flow

Side Hustle. Moonlighting. Night job. Passion project. The idea goes by many names, but the goal is the same—increase your income on a recurring or regular basis. Often this is in addition to your day job. It may grow out of a hobby or necessity.

First things first, don't do something you hate. Or even something you tolerate. This cash flow generator will be an activity that takes more time away from your family, so it damn well better be worth it.

Being a provider is *one* important aspect of fatherhood. But if working non-stop ends up being the only reason your kids will never remember you being at their games or recitals, you will have won one battle but lost the war. Keep it in perspective. Ensure your time providing is balanced with all the other events of the DadAthlon. Remember, even the fastest runner will never win the triathlon if he can't, or worse, *won't* swim or bike.

Goal Clarity

Before you take action, pause to determine your goal. Do you want this to be a side hustle that will *always* be a side hustle? Or are you looking to build something to *replace* your current job and throw off some extra cash until you're ready to go all-in? Knowing your goal is critical because you need to be realistic about the time and money invested on the front end relative to the upside on the back end. It does not make business sense to invest $10,000 to transform your hobby into a glorified cash flow hobby when it earns only a few hundred dollars a month. If you're doing it only for love, that's different. But also not a side hustle. Get clarity and be realistic.

But, if you do have a clear plan and commit to doing it right, you shouldn't be bashful about investing time and money to build the right skills and tools.

Two guys with the same day job and the same side-hustle plans may each take different paths depending on their goals.

Keep in mind, as with anything, there is no free lunch. Success is often proportional to input. If your goal is to make a ton of money and start a successful business, you'll likely need a large commitment. That is a calculation only you can make. One useful way to ensure you're balancing providing with your other priorities is to be completely clear on the time commitment required by this endeavor. Then add at least 50% as a margin of safety.

> Dad Hack: Balancing your time visualization: *Before* diving into a side hustle, take a moment to step back and imagine having a conversation with your *adult* children. Before you move forward in the present, clarify if the tradeoff is worth it to your *future* children. That is why you're doing all this, after all. So it makes sense to get their opinion. Ask *them* if they understand why you did this. Ask *them* if they think the cost was worth the tradeoff. In your mind, they are adults, so let *that* version of them come through. Were they able to go to college because you only went to one game per week instead of two? Or did they always have the newest iPhone but never saw you? Let them be honest.

Success Matrix

In his *7 Habits of Highly Effective People,* Stephen Covey observes that people often spend their whole lives climbing the ladder of success, only to realize that it is leaning against the wrong wall when they get to the top. I know the exercise above is a little squishy but imagining the present from the future perspective is a handy tool to ensure our most important ladder is planted firmly against the correct wall.

When deciding what the best option for you is, be sure to factor in these criteria—time, knowledge, location, and enjoyment. I call these elements the Success Matrix. The goal of this endeavor is to be successful, happy, and balanced. It's likely the most you will ever get by accident is two of those if you don't have a plan that checks off all four items on your personal Success Matrix.

I learned about the Success Matrix perspective from experience. I've been down this road. I have a job that I like and four kids who keep stubbornly getting older. But it turns out when you multiply average college tuition by sixteen—four kids for four years—you get a very large number very fast. So I was eager to supplement my day job with additional income as soon as possible.

I found several options over the years that I tried, but they all failed for several different reasons. Although I had reasonable expectations, I would have made better decisions had I run each plan through my Success Matrix first. So let's walk through each element together.

Time

How much time will doing this properly actually take? Be realistic about what it will take *and* how much time you are willing to spend. Assess the anticipated weekly time commitment. Also, be sure to factor in the short run and the long run. A plan may take a ton of time to ramp up—perhaps due to training or other logistics—but once the foundation is built, the time commitment dials back. It may be that a strategy takes twenty to thirty hours per week to build up in the first three to six months, then only six to ten per week after that. Be honest with yourself on the three variables below.

1) Short term weekly time commitment.
2) Long term weekly time commitment.
3) How many hours per week you, and your future adult kids, are willing to pay.

Knowledge

Some strategies require little to no additional knowledge. Others are very content-intensive, especially in various sub-segments of online opportunities. If you are side-hustling in your primary field, you may already be in decent shape. But if you are pursuing something different, be sure to acknowledge two things.

First, what you don't know you don't know is way bigger than you think. Lots of folks out there are doing a lot of things. The most successful people have spent tons of time learning and maintaining knowledge. Some of them have forgotten more than you will ever know. That is not necessarily a problem so long as you recognize it going in.

Second, and more importantly, you need to be interested in and enjoy your area of focus. Becoming successful in a new venture often requires a steep learning curve; you cannot afford for this to be a slog for you. You should have at least a general interest in the topic, if not a burning curiosity. This will get you through that dark hallway of exasperation when the excitement of the honeymoon wears off.

Location

Most options that get all the sexy press these days are laptop strategies—"work from anywhere!" These have obvious advantages, including the most obvious that they don't take you away from your kids. However, I invite you to contemplate two things.

First, if you choose a plan to be near your kids, but are always too busy on your laptop to engage them, perhaps you should rethink what it means to be present. Don't let the fact that you are geographically nearby replace the need to be *with* them when you are with them. It can be easy to rationalize that your geography is the only ingredient. Being down the hall but being unavailable may not be sufficient.

Second, there may be excellent options that don't require a steep learning curve or time away. An example might be something you do *with* your kids. Help *them* start a business mowing lawns or babysitting. Teach *them* how to manage their money well.

Enjoyment

Life is short. If you're going to pursue a side-hustle, *you* are in a position to pick what you want to do. For the love of God, stay away from stuff you hate. In fact, stay away from everything other than what you *love*. I tried a website-building business—I understood the business model, the marketplace, and the time commitment. I just hated digging into all the various techno-garble under the covers, which was necessary. I figured I could muscle through. But then found myself resenting this business I created.

Life is too short to spend *more* hours away from my family doing something I hate, fakely-justified that is it *for* them. Don't forget; *you* are the CEO of your life. Your best work will always be on the things you love doing. You're way better off focusing on a lower upside in an area you love than making yourself miserable pursuing riches in an area you hate or don't understand. Save yourself the time and the stress. Stick to the things you'd probably do anyway for free, then formulate a plan around monetizing the options in that space.

Ideas

Armed with the Success Matrix, it's time to find some concrete strategies that work for you. The list below is certainly not exhaustive, but these ten ideas will get you thinking about available options. Which ones fit well into *your* Success Matrix?

Start a Blog

Write about what you know and are passionate about. Blogs are easy and cheap to start, and you can do it anywhere. Good content providing valuable information to an engaged audience is vital if you want to monetize it. Income from blogs can vary greatly from a few hundred dollars a month to over six figures a year if done well and consistently. You may not make a ton of money out of the gates, but depending on your niche, time, strategy and expertise, a blog can become a steady source of supplementary income in time.

Affiliate Marketing

Much has been written on this topic. The idea here is that you sell other people's products to the audience you build. Paired with a blog on a niche topic can also be a nice source of income over time. The financial cost of going this route may not be large, but the time commitment can be hefty at first, especially if you are starting from scratch. The good news is that once you find something that works well, you can do this from anywhere.

Be a Virtual Assistant

You'll find several online platforms that match people who need stuff done with folks willing and able to do it. Virtual assistants (VAs) can do a broad range of tasks. Some of the most common include social media management, personal errands, booking travel, and helping manage calendars and events. But VAs can really end up doing just about anything. Depending on your time and skillset, this can be a useful and structured way to supplement your income. Several places worth looking into are:

Zirtual: https://www.zirtual.com/
PeoplePerHour: https://www.peopleperhour.com/
VANetworking: https://www.vanetworking.com/

Teach or Tutor

COVID has created two realities that create more opportunities for online tutoring. First is a broader acceptance and familiarity with the technology of online instruction. Second is a larger number of kids falling behind in certain classes and need specialized instruction to supplement standard school work.

Given home classes and the prevalence of Zoom, if you have specialized knowledge, you can easily find parents whose kids may need a little extra support with homework, especially in math, science, or foreign language. It helps if you have some educational background, but this could still be a good fit if you have specialized knowledge in a particular area.

What's your niche? Hook up with large-scale operations like tutor.com or care.com. Or, list your own services by spreading the word in your communities on Facebook or ask friends to forward along your skills. You can also post a job on Fiverr.com. Teaching English to international students can be a nice plug-n-play option. You don't need to speak Chinese but can make some extra money on a flexible schedule. Some of these programs require a bachelor's degree.

Tutor.com: https://www.tutor.com/
Care.com: https://www.care.com/
Teachaway.com: https://www.teachaway.com/schools/vipkid

Freelance Writing

If you enjoy writing and are good at it, many available options are worth looking into. A simple Google search for freelance writing jobs will turn up a large number of options. Some of these are bound to fit your skill-set and interest level. The Freelance Writer's Den is a good place to start. They are a membership community that offers both training and access to writing jobs. The time commitment depends on what type of writing you're interested in. As you might expect, most opportunities are very location flexible.

Gigs

These are just simple one-time jobs that you can do for people who need services—a bit like freelance writing but can be for anything. Fiverr and Upwork are two of the main places matching services with people who need them. Check out each site for the sorts of things folks offer online. They both have a very wide set of offerings. Examples include graphic design, writing sales copy, bookkeeping, tutoring, and voiceovers, among others. What do you do by day? What do you like? Search for that on these sites and see if you can do a little extra on the side of what you're already good at and enjoy. The time commitment is scalable given that you control how much or little you do, and the location is also very flexible for most options.

    Fiverr: https://www.fiverr.com/
    Upwork: https://www.upwork.com/

Local Jobs

This is similar to gigs above, but by definition, more local in nature. These are often related to a specific set of skills a provider has, especially regarding repair services. Some examples include handyman, furniture assembly, TV mounting, and hanging pictures. They can be gig-ish and one-time jobs like fixing a sink or repetitive, like mowing or shoveling snow. Other examples include dump runs, cleaning out garages, pet care, and music lessons. Seniors living at home in your area may be a good place for some of the home maintenance opportunities. Flyers at coffee shops or small ads in church bulletins are a good place to find possible customers, followed by word of mouth. Other jobs like this can be found on many websites, including the following.

Craigslist: https://www.craigslist.org/about/sites

Handy.com: https://www.handy.com/services. They require an application process, background check, and orientation. Often you need to have paid experience in the areas of focus.

Taskrabbit: https://www.taskrabbit.com/

Real Estate

I was hesitant to put this one on the list because it sounds so easy just to buy a place and collect passive income via rent. Reality, however, proves to be far more complicated and difficult. I include it because it *can* be a nice way to supplement your income but can *also* be a royal pain in the butt. Not to mention more costly than you think if you don't know what you're doing. This path requires extensive knowledge to do it well, so think twice unless you are dedicated to do it right or have a partner with the expertise to guide you through the jungle. In addition to time and knowledge, this option often requires money to invest and is obviously very location-specific. But done well in a good market, this can provide not only a stream of income but also growth as the value of your holdings appreciates.

Sell on Amazon

Buy products that you send to Amazon for them to fulfill. There are many books, YouTubers, and training programs eager to teach the basics. You'll need to factor in extra fees and research where to buy your products wholesale, among other things. While it is not quite as easy as it sounds, it is also not as difficult as you might fear and is doable with proper guidance. It will take time to ramp up and learn how to do it right. It also takes continuous effort to maintain and grow, but once you're up and running, this can produce a nice income, especially if you select popular products with good margins and play by the rules.

Driving – Uber, Lyft, or Doordash

Most folks know what this is. You drive people, and now *food*, around locally. You won't make a ton, and hours vary with your availability. This option works well if you have some hours to kill anyway and plan to catch up on your podcasts or audiobooks. This is also a good strategy if your day job's hours give you downtime while kids are in school. Single dads might also consider moonlighting while kids are with mom since it doesn't take you away from them. But, this can require a decent time commitment to make it worthwhile. Also, while aspects of this plan are specific to a location, some of the platforms will allow you to operate in cities or states other than your local area. Just make sure you understand each platform's rules before relying on that ability.

If you decide to move forward with any of the above, consider getting business cards. They'll give your side-hustle a more professional feel. Many easy options are available online. I've used Vistaprint, which has good deals on professional business cards as well as other printed products like flyers and brochures.

Summary

With our financial defense in order, a solid financial *offense* focuses on bringing dollars into the house.

Dollars are important, but not everything. It is critical to balance providing with being a father. Tailor your financial goals to achieve the specific things you want from life.

Strong financial offense includes both one-and-done strategies and side-hustles. The former focuses on one-time plans such as selling household items. The latter is intended to produce regular income streams in areas that check off all four boxes of your Success Matrix.

The Success Matrix helps you ensure that any side hustle you select is achievable and consistent with your bigger dad values. Analyze possible strategies by assessing their impact on your time, knowledge, location, and desire.

Do

- Get clear and specific on *why* you want to earn more—to save how much, for what, by when?
- Determine if your goals require a one-and-done solution or a steady higher cash flow.
- If one-and-done, pick a strategy and implement it. If you don't reach your goal, pick another and try that.
- If your goals require steady cash flow, determine your priorities in the Success Matrix. This ensures your plan addresses the requirements of time, knowledge, location, and enjoyment. Complete the Success Matrix Cheat Sheet to select a side-hustle that works well for you.

- Be realistic about how much time and effort you can allocate to your selected strategy.

Don't

- Put in place a strategy without thinking about it carefully first.
- Underestimate the time commitment your strategy will require.
- Do anything you hate.
- Ignore what your future kids would say about how *they'd want you to spend* your time.

PART 3
BREATHING EASIER - LIVING

> The really important thing is not to live, but to live well… and to live well means the same thing as to live honorably or rightly.
>
> – Socrates

> A sad soul can kill you quicker than a germ.
>
> – John Steinbeck

Many years ago, we took our kids to Disney World for vacation. The kids were the perfect age. They were overjoyed at the news we were going, and once we arrived, their eyes popped at every turn.

The days and lines are both long there, but my wife and I did our homework to minimize waits and maximize fun.

I have many great memories from that trip—from the Bibbidi Bobbidi Boutique to taking my five-year-old twins on The Bug's Life attraction. Spoiler alert: When the guide says a ride is scary for young kids, they are right. I still have fingernail scars in my arms.

One image I remember vividly, though, was from someone outside our family. My daughter and I were in line for the Mad Tea Party—the teacups—an oldie but a goodie. As we approached the front of the line, we watched the workers check all the cups to ensure everyone was safe. That's when I saw him. A dad was in one of the cups with his four-year-old daughter in a blue Cinderella dress.

Ahhh. Adorable.

Except it wasn't.

The daughter was looking left and right, giddily tapping him on the arm to show him all the wonders she saw.

And he was reading the Wall Street Journal.

He could not have been more unresponsive to his daughter if it were a stranger's kid sitting next to him on a subway.

On the God. Damn. Teacups!

…"and the cat's in the cradle and the silver spoon…"

I don't know what his job was. Maybe he needed market updates or was trying to multi-task by working a little over vacation. But I couldn't have been more struck by his tragic tone-deafness. How could he not see this moment more clearly?

Yes, we need to provide. Check.

We also need to connect with our kids, and we've discussed some strategies for that as well.

In the final analysis, though, we also need to be fully present in the *life* part of our lives, for our kids' sake as well as our own. We should be mentally and physically healthy enough to capitalize on a long life full of these opportunities. And ensure that we are fully and joyfully present for all of them so that we might better understand and convey to our kids real meaning and love.

This last section focuses on *living* well. In Chapter 8, we begin with tactics to lead healthy lives, inside and out. Chapter 9 stresses the importance of both creating and capturing joy for ourselves and our families. Finally, Chapter 10 delves into the value of pursuing and sharing wisdom.

CHAPTER 8

HEALTH

When health is absent, wisdom cannot reveal itself, art cannot become manifest, strength cannot be exerted, wealth is useless, and reason is powerless.

— Herophilus

I believe that the greatest gift you can give your family and the world is a healthy you.

— Joyce Meyer

You may have heard this one...

There was once a Countryman who possessed the most wonderful Goose you can imagine. For every day when he visited the nest, the Goose had laid a beautiful, glittering, golden egg.

The Countryman took the eggs to market and soon began to get rich. But it was not long before he grew impatient with the Goose because she gave him only a single golden egg a day. He was not getting rich fast enough.

Then one day, after he had finished counting his money, the idea came to him that he could get all the golden eggs at once by killing the Goose and cutting it open. But when the deed was done, not a single golden egg did he find, and his precious Goose was dead.

We have all likely heard Aesop's fable of the goose and the golden egg. The moral, of course, is that the pursuit of having it all right now destroys the very source of health and happiness, leaving you with nothing.

Imagine the sequel to the original story. Now armed with clear knowledge of that risk, having learned his lesson, the countryman would surely take better care of a second goose. He now knows that in the medium and short run, it is *much* better for him and certainly the goose to ensure the goose is adequately fed and nurtured. It's so clear it's almost laughable.

What does that have to do with us?

We are looking to cast the movie for this sequel to the Goose and the Golden Egg, and you are going to be in it. As a busy father trying to do it all, what role do *you* play in the sequel?

Trick question! You play *both* roles.

As dads, we have so much to do for work, mom, kids, school, sports, the house, college, the car, and the bills that we go go go nonstop. I can't let up for a second because before I married my wife, I promised her dad that I would take care of her. But I'm running late for the piano recital, and what time is her softball game, and the clothes are expensive, and that ER visit was a doozy, and how can I get these kids through college when it is so much even for just one! There is no time for rest; I must do more more more, and I forgot that I need a new timing belt for the car, and I want to take the kids to Disney next year, but the credit card balance is so high—and on and on and on.

And on.

And on.

No time to exercise. No time to breathe. No time to think. Just enough time to stress and keep my lips above the water. Then watch the clock slowly creep from two in the morning until I have to wake up at six, each moment thinking, *If I fall asleep right now, I'll still get three decent hours.*

Until the goose is dead.

Sound familiar? You are the countryman *and* the goose.

But in the sequel, we promised we'd take better care of the goose because no one gets what they want if we don't. Especially the kids.

What does taking care of your goose look like? Part of it is physical, to be sure. But we also need to balance social, emotional, and mental health.

Sure. Sucking it up and muscling through is one strategy, and many men, myself included, have said to themselves, *I don't have time to take better care of myself.*

Most of them even believed it.

Here are five reasons why that's bullshit:

1) Energy
   When you are healthy, you have a greater capacity to accomplish more of what you want. Good health and fitness create a growing inertia loop of energy and accomplishment. The better you feel, the more you do. The more you do, the better you feel. Thus, you don't have to start huge. Rather, start small and let it grow.

2) Fun
   When you are fit, you can actually *do* more of the things in life that are fun, especially with the kids. Skiing, running, playing basketball, laser tag—I underestimated its physical impact on a body until I still couldn't walk three days later! Good health allows you to be more active in your kids' lives and enjoy it along the way.

3) Example
   We all know our kids look up to us but are terrified to think they will imitate our worst habits. Spoiler alert: It's a package deal. Sure he has your cobalt blue eyes and rapier wit, but he will eat and drink like you as well. You tell me—is that a good thing for him? Behave like the adult you want your kids to be so that *they* have the long, energetic, fun lives you want *them* to have.

4) Your Priorities
   You can run, but you can't hide. When you do not have your health, it is much harder to accomplish the other valuable priorities in your life. Poor health saps both the time and energy required to deal with its consequences. That leaves less time and energy for the things you want to do. When you're not fit, you increase the degree of difficulty because so much of your "human RAM" is allocated to dealing with sickness or problems. It takes much less effort to stay ahead of life's ailments than to deal with them once they arrive. It is true that an ounce of prevention is worth a pound of cure. If you only have twenty ounces of energy in a day, it's tough to do all your worthwhile stuff when sixteen ounces are spoken for by "cure." Stay healthy, and you can allocate nineteen ounces to your priorities instead of four.

5) Being There
    Finally, here's the big one. Every father wants to walk his daughter down the aisle or see his son graduate or go fishing with his granddaughter. Life offers no guarantee; we all know that. But there are odds, as well as clear and statistically proven ways to improve them. So, if you want those things as much as your children want them, take good care of your goose to improve the odds.

Okay, we've covered the why. As for the how, that really isn't all that tricky. Most of us know exactly *what* we should be doing or avoiding. The hard part is deciding to do it and remaining consistent.

Body

We all know how to take better care of our bodies—eat well, move more. A vibrant, healthy body increases focused time and energy on our priorities. Many books explore both of those in detail, but below, we share a few high-level suggestions.

Refer back to our discussion of goals and habits in Chapter 5, and clarify a goal and create a simple plan to move forward. Pick *one* and start; remember to track your progress and celebrate your wins.

> Dad Hack: Fitness Apps: Here are a few useful apps and tools that have worked for me.
>
> My Fitness Pal: An app to set goals, easily track calories—in and out—and get info and support. The free version has all these features, and premium kicks them up a notch.

Zero Intermittent Fasting: An app to set goals and track hours between meals. Many types of fasts are available.

Beachbody on Demand: Tons of workouts and programs of every duration, intensity, and fitness level. Coaching as well. Not free, but well worth the cost and likely a lot less than your local gym.

Peleton: No, you don't need the bike. Like Beachbody, this membership has many types and styles of workouts you can do from anywhere with or without a bike.

Mind

Your body is a large part of your overall health, but it is not the only part. It's easy to fall into the same old patterns day after day. We often say, think, and do the same things without cultivating any new experiences or ideas.

Whatever you do, don't ossify into a stagnant uninteresting prick. Do what you enjoy, of course, but save some time to challenge yourself.

Read something new. Take up a hobby. Watch a weird movie, listen to a new band. Push yourself out of your comfort zone.

Especially if the new band or movie or book or idea is on one of your kids' playlists. Consider this a buy-one-get-one where you can connect with them by taking an active interest in what interests them.

That doesn't mean you'll end up liking or agreeing with it, but the *act* of doing that creates a connection between you. It also teaches—the kids and you—that good people can legitimately have different tastes and opinions and still be worthy of love and respect. Unfortunately, in this world of quick-hit, Twitter-fueled point-scoring, few people engage in any issue long enough to really understand it.

They peek under the covers *just* enough to discern whether it fits their present worldview, most often based less on merits than what others on their "team" think. At this point, they decide that either this person or idea is 100% cool, or this person or idea is 100% stupid and or evil.

The world is far more complicated, interesting and nuanced than 98% of people care to explore. Especially when it comes to "them"—the people we disagree with.

Chances are, "they" do the same cool/stupid/evil assessment of you.

Are you stupid? Or evil? Is there more behind your worldview than what can be understood in a tweet or a liked Facebook page?

Of course, there is!

Do you suppose that only applies to people who agree with you?

Curiosity > Judgment

If you haven't yet watched the show, *Ted Lasso,* I strongly recommend it. The show is hysterical and touching, both in the manliest of ways. Ted is an American football coach hired to coach a Premier League soccer club. Constantly underestimated throughout his life, he is affectionately nicknamed "Wanker" by his team's skeptical and deeply loyal fans.

There is a great scene in season one where the team's former owner challenges Ted to a game of darts over the rights to pick the lineup. Ted accepts only to discover his opponent, Rupert, has his own darts and is far more skilled than Ted may have thought.

As the game unfolds, Ted shares a story about the people who have always underestimated and belittled him. It used to bother him until one day when he saw a Walt Whitman quote painted onto a wall, "Be curious, not judgmental."

"All them fellas who used to belittle me, not a single one of them were curious. ...They judged everything, and they judged everyone. ...If they were curious, they'd ask questions. You know? Questions like 'Have you played a lot of darts, Ted?' To which I would've answered, 'Yes, sir. Every Sunday afternoon at a sports bar with my father from age ten till I was sixteen when he passed away.'"

With that line still hanging in the air, he casually tosses the winning dart.

Curiosity is not merely a soft, squishy nicety. Yes, of course, it is worthwhile to better understand other people—like your kids—for *their* sake. But curiosity > judgment is also pragmatic and useful. If Rupert were more curious, he would not have lost because he would not have played.

Where judgment creates blind spots, curiosity allows you to see around corners. Be curious about things outside your comfort zone—those you know nothing about and those you have problems with. That does not mean you need to agree with everything at the end of the day. But it does breed understanding, which is the key to better relationships, deeper knowledge, and greater success.

Not only will you enrich your mind, but you will do the same for your kids, who watch you pursue truth and seek to connect more honestly with them.

In addition to filling your mind with new and different ideas, *quieting* your mind is just as critical.

I know what you're thinking, and I've thought it too. But the word meditation has a lot of baggage it doesn't deserve.

For me, focused quiet time and intentional breathing grounds me at the beginning of my day. It can be as little as two minutes and as simple as setting a timer on your watch and breathing slowly.

Many apps and videos offer more guidance or structure. Some are aimed at general breathing; others focus on specific topics like goals, anxiety, or energy. The bottom line is these apps cost between nothing and next to nothing of both money and time. You can utilize them almost anywhere—like your car, bedroom, even on the toilet! They are effective at creating some calm and space to start or end your day. Some great resources to check out are Headspace, Simple Habit, Calm, and Insight Timer. YouTube is also a great place to search for free, but less structured options.

Heart

Men don't cry. Unless, of course, at a funeral or the Grand Canyon, in accordance with Ron Swanson's previously mentioned Pyramid of Greatness on the show *Parks and Recreation*.

Before you flip ahead, this is not a "get in touch with your emotions" section. There will be no trust falls or sharing circles. Those, of course, have their place, but for our purposes, we aren't concerned with them. Rather our concern here is to share two simple observations.

1) Your struggle is real.
2) Just like everyone else.

The takeaway from those observations is not "So suck it up and get on with your life." Rather, it's to illustrate that when managing life's stresses and difficulties, you need not bottle it all up inside until the only manly solution is a bottle from the outside.

An actual pressure tank builds pressure over time. Its most important feature is a pressure valve that lets *out* some steam now and then so that the whole thing doesn't explode.

We are all walking pressure tanks. But for some reason, men often think the pressure valve is not necessary. Or sometimes we let the pressure out in ways that aren't super healthy, akin to punching a hole in the tank with an ice pick. That solves the pressure problem in the short term but has its own long-term costs.

Take advantage of little ways to let the pressure out. Talk to your wife or your buddies. Be honest about what stresses you out and reflective about what you can do. Listen to your wife and buddies as well.

If that isn't something that works, grab a session once or twice a month with a therapist who can listen. In this post-COVID world, it has never been easier to get support without leaving your home or office. Most have remote or Zoom options now, and in addition, other options have been created for on-the-go support.

There is no shame in getting that support, and it doesn't mean you have a problem or you will get weird homework to do. Sometimes, the mere act of telling someone safe *everything* on your mind is itself therapeutic enough. Other times life offers us things you just can't tell your buddies or don't want to burden your wife with right now. Several years ago, I was in that situation and met with someone who listened as I vomited every last concern on my mind.

Honestly, for me, that metaphor is better than you think. When you have a bug, you don't want to throw up, but that feeling is telling you something is wrong. You sit in front of the toilet, both dreading it and wanting it over with as soon as possible. And once your system is purged, you start to feel better almost immediately. You can eat again.

I don't mean that metaphor at all disrespectfully to the mental health community. On the contrary, they help remove the toxins from our lives by providing a safe and judgment-free place to throw up. Sometimes my therapist provided strategies on how to handle things or different perspectives. Those were great, but honestly, that was a bonus. I mostly just needed a safe place to release the pressure.

> Dad Hack: Options for remote therapy. Dads are all very busy, and not having time to take care of the goose isn't just something we make up. Sometimes we need to find a solution that balances the needs we have with the time we have. Needing support no longer requires us to take a half-day off work. Technology now allows us to have our cake and eat it too. Options exist that provide fully trained and licensed psychologists and therapists that fit into our busy lives. These range from fully live sessions to text and audio support. We can get the assistance we need without leaving the house or even while we're commuting. Some good options to consider are:
>
> Better Help https://www.betterhelp.com/
> Talkspace https://www.talkspace.com/online-therapy/

Balance

Don't be a hero.

We dads have a lot to do and never enough time to do it. We *plan* to do ten pounds of stuff in a five-pound week. And when we *only* get six pounds done, we feel crappy, even though this is 20% more than what is realistic and healthy.

That "failure" stresses us out even more and makes us want to do more the following week and repeat the same cycle.

The irony is that we ignore all the golden eggs we produce, and over time feel crappier and crappier about all the eggs we are *not* producing. So we don't take any time to feed the goose because there *isn't any time,* dammit! I don't have time to feed the goose; I have too many eggs to make!

Until your goose is literally cooked and you die.

One skill many dads need to cultivate is balancing the eggs and the goose. Left unfettered, goose neglect only ends one way. It's very easy to see with the goose, but just as true with us.

Of course, there is a lot to do, but a few minutes each week to manage your task list thoughtfully reduces stress and keeps you moving toward your goals. As you do so, observe these five guidelines.

1) Plan your weeks.
2) Be realistic about what you can or should do in a given time.
3) Schedule downtime as part of your day or week the same way you would a dentist appointment.

4) Be kind with yourself when you fall short of your plans, but then…
5) Get back up and plan the next week.

> Dad Hack: Fill Your Tank Menu: Sure, I can plan downtime, but what the hell do I do with that time? Sit there and look at my laptop? The truth is, I have no clue what will work for you. We are all different and what works for one person may not for someone else. The key is to find out what works for *you* by trying several different ideas. Here are a few suggestions to get you thinking. What fills *your* tank? How do you feel after? Circle three or add your own. Put at least one on your calendar. Now.
>
> | | | |
> |---|---|---|
> | Exercise | Sit by the water | Video games |
> | Naps | Massage | Play with the dog/cat |
> | Sports | Movies by myself | |
> | Hunting | A nice lunch alone | Mow the lawn |
> | Fishing | Playing with my kids | Chop wood |
> | Hiking | | Whittle |
> | Reading | Sexy time with my wife | Social media |
> | Haircut (with a shave!) | | Stupid YouTube videos |
> | | Meditation | |
> | Go to a ballgame | Poker night with the boys | |
> | Quiet prayer | | |
> | Church | Driving | |

Resources

Now that we've discussed the importance of health and balance, below are a few concrete actions you can take. As discussed in Chapter 5, don't do them all at once. Think of these as a menu of options you can select from. Once you've finished one meal by installing it as a habit, come back to order another.

Routine

In Chapter 5, we talked about the importance of small habits. A good morning routine can help you be healthier and more effective. Start your day or end your day—eventually, maybe both—with a simple routine that helps you focus on the areas you decide are most important.

Begin with only one habit and keep it small, like exercise for five minutes or meditate for five minutes. Then after a couple of weeks, when that feels normal, if you want to add another one, go for it. You might work your way up to twenty minutes of exercise, five to ten minutes of meditation or prayer, two minutes of gratitude, and maybe even a few minutes to read or write.

Earlier I mentioned Hal Elrod's great book on the topic called *The Miracle Morning*, which I recommend. My only advice is to guard against making a grandiose morning routine the goal if that's not you. I once had a ninety-minute routine every morning, which was fine while it lasted, but hard to maintain with four school-age kids and a full-time job. I ended up having to scale it *way* back. The best routine is the one you will do consistently. Start small, but *stay* small if that works for you.

Meditation

Two to five minutes each morning or afternoon is all it takes.

Fasting

This ended up being much easier than I thought it was going to be. Again, I started small—basically just having breakfast later—and worked my way up. Many apps can help you track and plan. I used Zero and found it easy and effective.

Tracking Exercise

It has never been easier to see and celebrate your progress. Even if the thing you add is a walk every day. Refer to the Dad Hack above for a list of apps and platforms to try..

Hang Out With the Guys

Sometimes guys just need guys. My wife and her friends used to have a book club, and over a few drinks they'd discuss a book they'd read. Inspired by our wives' initiative, one of my buddies started a Gentleman's Book Club. Although I'm not sure the first two words were accurate, and the third was a little squishy since it's only loosely a "club." Primarily it offered a chance to just catch up over some beers and shoot the shit. If COVID has taught us anything, it is the mental health value of getting together with people we like and sharing stories, refreshments and laughter.

Humor

Speaking of laughing, I believe laughter is a critical part of maintaining one's health. Find and *create* opportunities to laugh. With your buddies. With your wife. With your kids. By yourself, even! I'm ashamed to admit how many Steve Harvey Family Feud outtakes

I've chuckled at quietly to myself as I'm winding down my day watching dumb crap on YouTube! I think finding and creating joy is so important to a person's or family's success that it has its own chapter. Stay tuned…

Summary

If dads do not prioritize time to feed their goose, they sacrifice present happiness and risk missing out on much more through illness or death.

Men must plan time to nourish their bodies, minds, and hearts. These don't need to be giant activities but can be small strategies easily woven into the fabric of our lives.

Many apps and resources make this process simple and effective.

Do

- Take time to feed your goose.
- Schedule a real appointment in your calendar to do something that fills your tank.
- Implement one small habit into your morning that supports an area of need: body, mind, or heart.
- Once it's second nature, implement another.

Don't

- Overbook your schedule.
- Kill your goose.

CHAPTER 9

JOY

The mass of men lead lives of quiet desperation.

– Henry David Thoreau

Let your joy be in your journey—not in some distant goal.

– Tim Cook

Not long after our twins were born, we went on a road trip for the holidays from our home in Minnesota to my in-laws in Cleveland. Our twins were three months old, and our oldest had just turned two. It was a turbulent and deeply sleepless time in our lives. Although we knew the trip would be difficult, we were eager to see family. Perhaps we were also desperate to have other humans help with these tornados of adorability.

My wife was nursing the twins, which complicated the drive a bit. During the day, they needed to eat every three and a half hours, and the full process took an hour each time. That may not be a big deal on a three-hundred-mile drive because you only need to stop once. But on an eight-hundred-mile drive, that adds a *lot* of time. So we decided to take the highway red-eye and drive through the night. That way, we could stretch the time a little longer between feedings and have one or two fewer stops. That may not sound like a lot, but on the margin, that was huge!

We left Minnesota at four in the afternoon, thinking that after stops, we would maybe pull into my in-laws around eight or nine in the morning. They could then watch the kids while we napped for a bit. Things worked well. We stopped around seven and again around half-past ten. To our amazement, the twins slept over *six* hours after that late evening meal until just before five the next morning. The plan was working since we could now make it the rest of the way without a fourth or fifth stop.

When we stopped, we followed a thoughtful process to ensure everyone was fed and cleaned efficiently. We always stopped at McDonald's because, at the time, our experience was that it was the only national chain that *always* had a changing table in men's rooms. I would take the twins in first and change them. Then I'd bring them back out to the car, where my wife would feed them while I took our oldest into the bathroom. Then order food for everyone, then return to the car to help burp and settle the twins while my wife went inside for a few minutes. Clockwork.

Like many two-year-olds, my older daughter was very curious and eager to explore this wonderful new world of language. She wasn't yet ready for the toilet, so I had her on the changing table when a gentleman walked in to use the urinal.

Now I should pause here to say that when we first began talking to our kids about their private areas, we simply called everything your "hiney." Front or back, boy or girl, all of it was your hiney. I know. You're supposed to use accurate anatomical language. But our oldest was still only two, and we were operating on fumes, just making sure they all ate and slept. Enlightened language for one's privates was not on our priority list.

As this man walks up to the urinal while I'm changing her, my ever-curious, super-squirmy daughter is arching her back to take a closer look and say hello. At which point, she becomes startled, looks up at me in amazement, and shout-whispers, "Daddy! That man has a *hot dog* in his *hiney!*"

…

Uhm…

Awkward does not begin to describe it.

I am at a total loss for words and sheepishly turn my head, hoping Mr. Hot Dog somehow didn't hear or had headphones in or something.

Nope.

But to my relief, he was chuckling. "Sorry, man," was all I could muster.

And just as the awkwardness was dissipating a bit, my proud, curious little girl chimes in with, "I don't have a hot dog in *my* hiney. I have *pancakes!*"

Ah, the world through the eyes of a two-year-old girl. I bet that's how they teach it in medical school.

At that moment, I was deeply and profoundly embarrassed by this unusual exchange we accidentally inflicted on a stranger.

Moments later, though, I realized this was a ridiculous interaction that I would treasure forever. A story I love sharing to this day, *especially* in the presence of my daughter! Turnabout is fair play, of course.

At the end of the last chapter, we touched on the value of laughter from a health perspective—how laughter itself is not only fun but therapeutic. In this chapter, we expand a bit on that and discuss how dads should both capture and create joy wherever possible. Joy is such an important part of health for your kids and you that it gets its own chapter.

Much has been written about the physiological benefits of laughter. Countless studies observe its positive impact on stress, blood flow, immune system, pain, and mood.

Plus, obviously, life is more enjoyable and fun, memories are happy, and people enjoy each other's company more. Finding and creating joy is good for the body, the mind, and our relationships. In a sense, this also weaves through all the other events. It helps us better deal with the stress of the logistics and facilitates connections with our daughters, sons, and wives.

We all know how to be happy when fun things come our way. However, this chapter focuses on two things that do not occur automatically—creating and capturing joy.

All of us are certainly able to feel joy and laugh when funny things find their way to us. But why wait? Most dads implicitly understand their need to insert a little humor into their family's lives. The fact that "dad jokes" are a thing at all is a testament to that! The goal here is to find a few simple ideas to make joy happen on purpose more often in the lives of our families—to *create joy* proactively.

While many happy or funny experiences come and go throughout our lives, most of them just slide away. We remember a few funny stories, but many get lost in the ether or become hard to share with others. So, it's essential for us to take the time to capture more of those moments easily and simply in a way that allows us to continue to experience the joys we have already seen. Whether we create the joy or it finds us, technology today makes it easier than ever before to capture the joy effectively.

Let me pause for a moment. I am not suggesting that any of this means that moms do not create or bring joy. But joy comes in different flavors, and both are a critical part of the balanced breakfast of childhood. Mom joy is often steady, reflective, nurturing, and warm. In our house, dad joy is usually more physical, goofy, quick-hitting, and sometimes embarrassing.

Create joy

Almost subconsciously, dads look to create opportunities for fun, humor, or memories—often served with a side of embarrassing a kid or two. The desire to make silly comments in front of kids' friends, lean into the lame pun, and even throw that toddler up in the air *just* a little farther than mom thinks is safe all come hard-wired in most dads. Creating these opportunities for joy is crucial.

Our goal here is to share a few concrete ideas for dads who want to find and remember fun and laughter with their families. Some of them are obviously more for little kids and others for all ages

Experiences

I'm not talking about planning giant trips to Wally World, which, while certainly *intended* to create joy, can sometimes backfire a bit. Vacations and trips are fun but can also be stressful and taxing. The two things I'd suggest in the big vacation bucket are buy-in and downtime.

Whether you're going to Paris for a month or camping for a weekend, try to give each kid—or at least each one old enough to complain—some agency in part of the experience. So that *they* get to create part of the joy that becomes the family trip. However, that doesn't mean they plan the whole thing or get to veto giant swaths of it. But even something as simple as "pizza or Chinese" can give them a sense of ownership and investment that they can feel proud of. Moreso, anyway, than if every minute of every hour, from their perspective, is orchestrated from on high.

Many vacations are lots and lots of downtime, which is great. But some others are on the move. Rides to ride, pictures to take, strange overpriced foods to eat. On such trips, I've found that cramming day after day after day of *vacation dammit* can itself be rather taxing on all.

Yes, you spent a lot to get here, and you'll be damned if you waste a day sitting around the hotel pool while there are lines to wait in! But it's often a good idea to take a day or even just a morning to sleep in and chill. This becomes more critical as your kids get older. Maybe you can get a buy-one-get-one, and the older kids can pick what day is chill day and what to do after?

Buy-in and downtime on large vacations may not look like they *create* joy, but they protect the joy created all around them.

My main focus in this chapter is to look for smaller, easier experiences to create. Some of your bigger wins may even become family traditions your *kids* want to keep doing. The sorts of things they will always look back on fondly.

Outside

Head to the local little league field for a whiffle ball or kickball game. My brother-in-law did this one year on Memorial Day weekend. He invited a few of his kids' friends' families for a simple impromptu game and included us. All we brought was a ball and some drinks. Now we do it every year. Stuff like this checks off a few boxes—exercising, fun, tradition, with friends. Near the end of May every year, my kids ask, "Are we doing the kickball game again this year?" Nailed it, Uncle Paul!

The Sky

Keep your eyes peeled for the next lunar eclipse or meteor shower. Wake the kids up—or let them *stay* up—then take them outside and see this rare event. It will be cold but grab blankets, hot chocolates, lay down in the grass, and look up together. You may end up seeing nothing. But here's the thing—that makes a good story too.

> Dad Hack: The Perseid Meteor shower is an annual event. It typically peaks around August 12 every year as the earth passes through the same debris from the Swift Tuttle comet. You'll see more action before dawn than in the late evening because the earth's rotation will be the same direction as its motion through space, which means the sky passes through more meteors as it moves through the field more quickly. Now you can plan accordingly.

Stories

Build a fire and tell stories. There are many variations on this, so stick with me. Mom and dad can tell all the stories. While "normal" stories like Goldilocks and her travails may be popular, "real" stories, especially ones about mom and dad when they are younger, are always crowd-pleasers. How did mom and dad meet? What were grandma and grandpa like when you were a kid? Especially popular are stories about funny or embarrassing events from years past. This is particularly fun for the kids if uncles or aunts are there to fill in the information gaps mom and dad purposely left out.

Scary stories are also always a fun option. I know what you're thinking, "I don't *know* any good stories."

Three solutions:

1) Online: C'mon, Dude! Has Google taught you nothing? If you don't know any, you can find a few to get you started at these links:

    https://koa.com/blog/kid-friendly-spooky-campfire-stories
    https://icebreakerideas.com/campfire-stories

2) Kids: Often, kids have silly, weird or scary stories of their *own* they want to tell. Maybe something they heard at school or scouts or, if you're lucky, they made up themselves and can't wait to share with pride. And which we as parents love to listen to with pride. And maybe sometimes concern…

3) Improv: Some of the funniest stories we ended up with were simply collaborative efforts where the kids wanted to keep storytime going, but we were all tapped on material. So we told a story together where each person can only tell

one sentence. Then the next person has to pick it up from there. Things get weird and funny fast. If you're particularly adventurous, limit each contribution to one *word*.

If the above options don't work for you or you've already done them, set up a movie in the backyard on a screen for your kids and their friends. Use a sheet and borrow a projector from work or a buddy. Large or inflatable screens are also available online for about a hundred dollars if you make it a recurring event. Paired with s'mores and blankets, this is a real crowd-pleaser for kids.

Holidays

Holidays are a great example of where dads can hit the unholy trifecta of laughter, eye-rolling, and traditions—with a potential bonus of scaring neighborhood kids. If you are the "answer the door" parent on Halloween, dive in with both feet, and get creative. A ridiculous or clever costume is a great start, but no need to stop there. There are some great ideas on this site to check out: www.DadAthlon.com/Joy. You've done it right if you become "that house" in your neighborhood.

Every 4th of July, my father-in-law divides the families and kids into two teams to compete in a bunch of Minute-To-Win-It games. It has become quite a competition among the kids. The teams change each year, but every one of them looks forward to it.

Scavenger hunt or geocaching is also fun. You can set up small yard-based scavenger hunts for little kids and their friends. Or work with a group of friends whose houses or an item at their houses is the target. Each home writes a clue, which spreads the effort out a bit. We did this for a few birthday parties, and it worked well.

Also, geocaching is a larger scale option for whole families or even breaking into teams to get through several near you. It gets you outside; you work together, see cool stuff—sometimes lame stuff—and the best part is that all the hard work is already done for you! Just signup and start looking for hidden treasures near you. www.Geocaching.com has an app you can download, create a profile and use for free. Find easy ones, hard ones, ones hidden in the woods or in the city. There is a premium option, which to no one's surprise, has more features. But even that is much less for a year than taking your kids to a movie or dinner. You can sort by difficulty or terrain and even see which ones are tagged as favorites most often by other users.

Concerts

As you get to know what music your kids like, look for concerts in your area or make a trip out of it and visit your closest big city. Follow artists on Ticketmaster or Livenation for well-known acts or if your kids' tastes are more niche, check out www.Bandsintown.com or www.bandcamp.com.

Or perhaps your community has local restaurants that have live music—this can be a low-cost alternative. Concerts or not, the act of getting to know the music your kids like is itself a nice way to connect on car rides, especially for teens. I can't tell you how often I've gotten in the car, and their headphones go in before the seatbelt goes on. I'll ask, "Hey, you want to play your music through Bluetooth?" Sometimes the answer's been no thanks, but other times I've gotten through large swathes of their playlist, and they like talking about their bands. I do my best to remember some of the names and toss them into one of the above sites, but band names these days… Am I right? Whether the band is The Rolling Stones or Slaughter Beach, Dog, music is a great way to connect.

Comedians

If your kids are on the older side, watching comedians instead of TV shows or movies is a great option. While some comedians have reputations for being mostly clean (Jim Gaffigan, Jerry Seinfeld, Brian Regan, to name a few), many others are well worth considering if you do a little homework. Hour-long specials are all over streaming services, including, I'm sure, one of the three *you* have. In addition, YouTube has plenty of shorter sets and compilations for free. These are a fun and easy way to laugh together and often lead to family inside jokes as the kids sometimes repurpose material into crazy episodes of your lives. *Plus*, these guys tour as well, making their concerts another fun option.

> Dad Hack: Family-friendly comedians. You may know a few of these names already, but here is a list of very funny comedians you can watch with your kids. Some are young, others have been around a while, but funny is funny. Preview them on YouTube or a streaming service first to verify that they are *your* kind of clean and also that you think they are funny: Jim Gaffigan, Brian Regan, Jerry Seinfeld, Ellen Degeneres, Bob Newhart, Nate Bargatze, Bill Engvall, Ryan Hamilton, Michael, Jr. The Carol Burnett Show

Dad Jokes

Speaking of humor, no chapter on dad-sponsored joy would be complete without a comment on dad-jokes. Embrace your inner nerd and use that power for groans instead of evil! Deploy them often. Do not back away. If their eyes aren't rolling, you're not trying hard enough. Two strategies here:

1) Premeditated: The DJOTD—dad joke of the day—which is a great option for breakfast, before school, or written on a family whiteboard every day. Plenty of websites exist to give you ideas. It's impossible to fail here. Google or Alexa can also offer quick and easy results.
2) On the Fly: This one is more of a life skill, though no one has ever called it that. Ever. But you'll recognize your opportunities to pounce as you come across them in your daily conversations.

Finally, rather than plan all of the above in secret, let them see you looking for things to do with them and for them. Better yet, whenever possible, make them a part of the process. This teaches them that you love them enough to spend time creating joy for or with them, and it models excellent behavior for when they have their own kids.

These are only a few ideas on how to manufacture joy and memories for your family. This list is not intended to be exhaustive but simply offers a few easy things you can do to start; it primes the pump.

Your kids will carry memories of your activities with them throughout their lives and maybe even use a few of them for *their* families. Your act of proactively creating opportunities for joy itself sets an example for them in their lives.

Capture Joy

I don't know about you, but I sometimes listen to stories my kids tell about things we've done as a family. While I may remember *being* there, I have nowhere near the detail that they do. Maybe I'm just old. Or perhaps there is already too much stuff taking up my mental RAM to have space to store what flavor the ice cream was or which shirt mom was wearing when we laughed at that giraffe peeing at the zoo. While those specific details may not be mission-critical to a fulfilled life, it's enough to wonder what else I may be missing. We spend so much time creating these joyful experiences; it sure would be nice to be able to look back on them years later and see them in technicolor.

Warning: Don't make capturing the joy overshadow creating it. Fun experiences aren't quite as fun when it's all about smiling for the camera. So take pictures or videos, but don't be *those* parents, so focused on capturing the moment that the camera *is* the moment. Balance is a tricky thing to achieve. Hell, it's damn near the whole point of this book. But capturing joy is about more than merely taking pictures. This section explores a few ways to have our cake and eat it too.

Write

The process of writing things down captures memories in a way that pictures and videos can't. Write for others or write for yourself. You can go big or little here.

Writing for others might take the form of social media posts. Tweets are punchy and easy, or even a blog—way bigger than tweets—is pretty easy to do too. Crazy stuff your kids say or do could supply enough subject matter for either a Tweet series or a blog.

Another example of writing for others is annual holiday letter updates. Updates are great, but find a way to make it silly. You probably get a ton of holiday letters—which ones do you read first? Why? Capture the year, but capture the joy also.

One specific circumstance where writing for others is valuable is if you live far away from loved ones, especially grandparents, and want to ensure they're plugged into your lives. When our twins were born, we lived nearly 1,000 miles away from our families and started a blog to keep them in the loop—and maintain our sanity. Looking back now, fifteen years later, it is a gift that we captured those silly stories. They are also fun to share with older versions of the kids, who each love to hear about what a holy terror they were!

That is a nice segue into another audience you can write for—future *you*. You can even keep it simple, like a bullet journal with just a sentence or two a day. You might reflect on things other than your kids, but at least reflect regularly on what happened.

So write. *For you* may someday be *for others.*

Tell stories that celebrate the kids, their silliness, their creativity, their energy. Try to get past droning on about how well they did in little league or grades on a test. And not something that makes fun of them, but something that celebrates a story about them, especially funny stories that they love—like the hot dog in the hiney.

Pictures and Videos

Review old pictures from time to time. Schedule one day a year to comb through your computer and phone. Charge up those old phones and blackberries you had before everything synced in the cloud. Doing this as a family over or after dinner is a wonderful alternative to TV or devices and can remind you of silly stories to write down—as mentioned above! It makes for a fun night. Seeing events like these through your kids' eyes is often eye-opening and hysterical.

Combine family photos with a gift for mom, for Mother's Day, or her birthday. Most computers have software that makes it easy to compile an automatic slideshow that can be snazzed up with minimal effort.

If you have an abundance of videos, the above two ideas work just as well. Like with the pictures, stitch your videos into a short movie for mom or grandma, or future you or future kids! Use cool transitions and nice music. You can do a basic job on your own with video editing software or really amp it up with an expert's help. There are thousands of folks out there ready to solve your problem for you and knock your socks off editing your videos into a kickass Mother's day gift for a low price. Check out Fiverr or Upwork for plenty of options that cost less than you think. Search "home video editing" and go to town.

Summary

Joy is therapeutic and memorable. Good dads don't wait for joy to find their family; they proactively look for ways to create joy. Experiences, activities, and stories are great ways to purposely create joyful memories for your family.

Once created, it's also important to capture the joy in writing, pictures, videos. These memories will be treasures for you, your kids, and even others outside your family.

As with everything, balance is key.

Do

- ➤ Seek out opportunities for memories.
- ➤ Celebrate our kids with stories about them *to* them and *for* them.
- ➤ Capture memories in writing, pictures, and videos.
- ➤ Let your kids *see* you being proactive about creating joy in their lives.

Don't

- ➤ Make jokes at your kids' expense.
- ➤ Wait to write down your memories and stories.
- ➤ Be *so* concerned about capturing the joy that you're not living the joy—or worse, ruining it for the kids!

CHAPTER 10

WISDOM

> I believe that what we become depends on what our fathers teach us at odd moments when they aren't trying to teach us. We are formed by little scraps of wisdom.
>
> – Umberto Eco

A long time ago, before I had kids, I was talking to a parent who said, "We're not raising our son in a faith tradition; we want to let him choose when he is old enough. We don't know everything and want him to be able to discern for himself."

I remember at the time thinking, "Wow, that seems really odd. I bet that takes guts and, perhaps ironically, faith." Not being a dad yet, though, I deferred to his age, experience, and wisdom. I figured that when the babies start arriving, the magic dad-texts we'd all receive would clearly validate this approach. I convinced myself that I respected his intellectual humility as well as his protection of his son's autonomy.

Now I am older than he was then, with more kids than he had then, who are themselves older than his kids were then. And it turns out

I *still* think it is really odd. But this time, I do not need to defer to his age and wisdom.

I still do agree with his reasons—humility and autonomy. But I think his *reactions* to those beliefs missed a critical opportunity for dad-ness—imparting wisdom.

Like him, I deeply admire intellectual humility *and* respect the autonomy of all people, especially my children. But if age teaches anything, it is that we often know less than we think. That humility and the knowledge we have forged from our mistakes can build a foundation for our kids. It is ballast upon which they are able to perceive the world with greater clarity and adjust accordingly.

There is much to know and understand in this complex world. Whatever your faith approach is or isn't, it is almost certainly the product of struggles and lessons. Your approach may not be perfect.

Spoiler alert: it isn't. A*nd* neither is anyone else's.

But to allow a child to discern her own faith untethered from your own guidance is to abdicate one of the most important roles that every parent and dad must fill—*teacher.*

Interestingly, few people have this approach elsewhere in life. We don't know everything there is to know about food production or nutrition. But we respect our son's autonomy, so should we let him make his own decisions and be a candytarian?

There are many languages in the world, some more efficient or poetic than others. But we do not avoid teaching *any* language so that our daughter can decide which she wishes to speak. She needs to learn *some* language in order to be equipped to even make the decision.

Why then would it make sense to punt on the very essence of life, existence, and meaning? Regardless of our specific beliefs, why would we pick *that* issue to teach them nothing under the banner of humility and autonomy?

You know more than your child does. You might be wrong. He or she might eventually disagree with you. Both are fine. In fact, you may disagree with your younger self! But you *do* have knowledge, wisdom, and experience that your kid needs to learn from, even if only from your mistakes.

On the bicycle of life's wisdom, you need to be moving in some direction, any direction, before you can steer. Teach the direction that you do know. *Then* be open to their autonomy. They or you may need to turn. Allow them to challenge you as they grow in knowledge and their own wisdom.

If we do not teach our children, we sentence every future generation to start from scratch by themselves on the things that matter most.

Teaching our children wisdom is our last event. Faith is part of wisdom, but certainly not all of it. Wisdom encompasses more than faith alone; it includes our own life lessons, learned from our parents, gleaned from life, and forged by our own failures.

When it comes to your faith tradition, unlike my friend's approach above, we should *teach*, talk, and live our faith. When they are younger, pass it along. If nothing else, give them something to challenge, which will only improve your own proximity to the truth. If you have no faith tradition but want one for your kids, don't be afraid to walk the road together.

As your kids grow, they will have questions, many of which will be much more profound and insightful than you will expect. Don't punt when they approach you. *Talk* with them. Answer their questions as best as you can. Say you don't know when you don't know, and look for the answers together. Some questions, especially the hard ones, may not have answers, which is itself a lesson. Don't bullshit your kids. That's a good rule in general, but especially on the topic of faith and wisdom.

Finally, while you are teaching and talking, be sure you live your life in a way that is congruent with your faith and conversations. Kids know when the audio doesn't match the video; don't give them a reason to think you're full of crap. You're their dad and supposed to be the most reliable source of truth and wisdom. Teach and talk and live it.

Capturing wisdom

As with capturing joy above, it's also important to collect everything you do want to pass along. Like a nice dream that evaporates two minutes after you wake up, those valuable nuggets will disappear quickly. Don't let them.

Capturing them doesn't need to be a large or complex endeavor. You can do something as simple as writing a few notes in a journal. You can even use the voice memo app on your phone to capture quick nuggets that occur to you on the fly. Schedule time with yourself once a week/month/quarter to gather this stuff together. Maybe you end up making it into a book for your kids. Or possibly it stays in a journal.

You might turn your nuggets of wisdom into a note or a slide show for your kids as they go off to college. Your new friend on Fiverr could edit pictures of your children with wisdom bombs voiced over by you.

But What the Hell Do I Write About?

You know. Or, more accurately, you'll know when it dawns on you. Your phone almost certainly has a simple "notes" app. Capture placeholders there for the things that pop into your head as you navigate the world. Notice the things you or others do that are heart-warming. Or aggravating; or one part might include a few lists, such as *never do this* or *be sure you do that*.

Jot down your life lessons—what have you learned? My list includes the following nuggets.

- ➢ Seek truth always: curious > judgment.
- ➢ Do what you love.
- ➢ Be kind.
- ➢ Work hard.
- ➢ Don't fear mistakes or failure.

These few nuggets aren't magic secrets, nor is this list even remotely exhaustive. But magic beans only grow when you plant them. For these ideas to truly take root in your kids' lives, you must plant them in the soil of your own experiences and stories.

This is especially true if you learned your lesson by failing to do these well. However you capture or convey your wisdom, do your best to make it *your* wisdom.

The items in the above list are certainly worthwhile. But any of them can be something any human says to any other human any day of the week. What makes it powerful for kids is the proximity, credibility, and authority of these nuggets when glued to a story their dad told them.

When You Speak...

Mind your words carefully. In the ears of our children, they are more powerful—positive *and* negative—than we can possibly imagine. Your kids may not always want you to know that, but it's true.

Tell them the truth always. If a particular scenario is not appropriate or none of their business, simply tell them that. They may not like that either, but the cost of bullshitting them is far higher.

When you make a mistake, are wrong, or are a jerk, either to them or someone else, especially their mom, own it. If you are in the wrong, don't simply let everything passively cool off, and then in a day or two, everyone forgets. Take the bull by the horns and proactively make it right, especially if the one you have wronged is your kid. They know you are not perfect.

Taking responsibility is not only healthy for your relationship, but it also models mature interactions. As your children grow, they often pay way more attention to what you *do* than what you say—*especially* if there is a disconnect between the two. Tell them about the lessons you've learned from the mistakes you've made.

Pursue Wisdom

So far, we have discussed wisdom you have gleaned along the way on the journey of life. You are a father, but you are a man first, with your own journey. Sometimes wisdom finds you, but part of acquiring wisdom is pursuing it.

Have real conversations with people about real things. It may not always be a great fit at work or at the bar, but don't be bashful about life, faith, fear, meaning, loss, and joy, especially with a group of good pals or siblings or your wife.

If you're lucky enough to have your dad in your life still, reach out to him. What does *your* dad wish he knew when he was your age? What does he know now that would matter most to you? Have you ever asked him? I bet he'd love to answer that. Or try your father-in-law or a friend's dad.

Wisdom is a lifelong journey, and we are all at different spots along the way. We must not only actively *seek* directions from those in front of us but also share guidance with those behind us.

Notice what you read, listen to, and watch. Life is full of hard questions about real issues. Loss. Suffering. Meaning. Even God. It's arrogant to think any one person can figure it all out on their own. There is so much out there worth understanding, curated over centuries of wisdom. The more I find, the more I realize, the more there is to find.

But here's the thing—wisdom is not going to find you. Books don't have legs. But today's technology offers the next best thing. A few keystrokes are all it takes.

What issues are you most curious about or struggling with? Google "best books on wisdom," suffering, meaning, or joy. You'll get many hits. Pick a few. On Amazon, you'll also see related titles and reader reviews, which help narrow it down. The key here is not so much where you look for these or how you look, but *that* you look.

Some folks prefer listening to reading. Most of the books you find will also have audio versions. I'm a longtime member of Audible.com.

If books are too long, podcasts are a great quick-hit alternative. They cover every topic under the sun. Search for a couple that fit your area.

YouTube is also an excellent source of easy-to-consume wisdom. Of course, it can also be a vast wasteland of weirdness. A well-crafted search on your topic will produce quality results for you to pick from. Videos last from two minutes to two hours. The bonus is that YouTube displays other related content, which may help you hone in on your need.

Finally, no discussion of books and wisdom would be complete without sacred texts. Whatever your faith tradition, these sources are often bursting with wisdom. The issue is most often that people never really engage them. Many are complex, with layers of meaning and eons of ancient context. If the texts themselves are daunting, books *about* the texts might be a softer alternative and a good place to start.

As we strive to pass along wisdom to our kids, most of what's valuable boils down to three basic principles.

We must ensure that the actions we take in our lives are consistent with the things we say. When there is a disconnect, our kids will know it, and it can damage both your relationship and image in their eyes

The things we say, though, should have value, depth, and truth. The weather and the ball game are helpful and fun, but there should be substance to our lives that runs deeper than superficial activities.

Finally, we should live our lives with intention. Life is too short, and our kids are too important to merely react to the noise of the world. Thoughtfully determine what is important to you, make a plan to find it, and walk boldly in that direction.

In a nutshell, the key to dad wisdom—and all the events of the DadAthlon—is simple.

Do what you say.

Say what you mean.

Mean what you do.

Summary

Wisdom is a vital component of a life lived well. As both fathers and men, we should seek wisdom for its own sake and teach what we have learned to our kids.

Faith is one aspect of wisdom we should teach, talk, and live. Discussing faith and wisdom candidly with our kids can be difficult but worth it.

Capturing wisdom is essential to our personal growth and for passing along the lessons we've learned.

Countless resources are available to dads who want to pursue wisdom—our fathers, books, sacred texts, podcasts, and YouTube, to name a few.

The key to dad-wisdom is to do what you say, say what you mean, and mean what you do.

Do

- Teach your kids about your faith.
- Talk to them about your failures and what you learned.
- Own your mistakes and take responsibility, both with them and with others in front of them.
- Capture the wisdom you've acquired in your life—for you *and* your kids.
- Finally:
    - Do what you say.
    - Say what you mean.
    - Mean what you do.

Don't

- Bullshit your kids.
- Shrug your shoulders on life's most important questions.
- Be passive.
- Avoid hard conversations with your kids on real issues just because you may not have a good answer.

PART 4
NOW WHAT?

CHAPTER 11

GAME TIME

> People may doubt what you say, but they will believe what you do.
>
> – Lewis Cass

> Well done is better than well said.
>
> – Benjamin Franklin

> Inaction breeds doubt and fear. Action breeds confidence and courage. If you want to conquer fear, do not sit home and think about it. Go out and get busy.
>
> – Dale Carnegie

Throughout this book, we've explored many ideas and actions to help you round out the muscle groups you think need work.

In the first section on loving better, we focused on the essential skills of connecting with those most important to us. Chapter 2 laid out many ideas and resources on connecting with our daughters, and in

Chapter 3, our sons. Chapter 4's emphasis was our primary parenting partner, suggesting ideas and strategies to ensure she and we feel supported, appreciated, and heard.

In the next section on doing more, we turned our attention to the logistical and stressful elements of planning and providing for life's necessities. Chapter 5 dug into execution, with insights into setting and achieving goals while focusing on one thing at a time. Chapter 6 on financial defense laid out specific plans and strategies for protecting money going *out* the door, while Chapter 7 outlined both one-time and recurring ideas on ways to bring more money *in* the door creating a financial offense.

In the final section on living well and breathing easier, we pivoted to those moments that make life worthwhile. These will be a source of wisdom and guidance for our families both while we are with them and long after we're gone. Chapter 8 laid out strategies for maximizing our physical and mental health. Chapter 9 delved into the value and options for creating and capturing joy. And Chapter 10 highlighted the simple lessons of life by seeking and sharing wisdom.

Let's return for a moment to that image of your 80-year-old self. Looking back on your life as it played out on your current trajectory, what would your 80-year-old self wish you did differently? Spend more quality time with your daughter? Create fun family memories together? Have more real conversations with your kids about faith or life or death? Waste less money on stupid things that aren't important? Like George Bailey or Scrooge, this exercise gives you a glimpse into a possible future outcome, one which *might* become a reality.

As the not-so-subtle quotes that begin this chapter suggest, talk is cheap. Now it's time to shape your future's past by taking action in the present.

You might not be exactly sure where to begin. Which event is most important? When you ride a bicycle, you need to be moving before you can steer. Move first. Steer later.

Start with the Dad Quiz at www.DadAthlon.com/DadQuiz to get clarity on your highest priority area. Implement *one* strategy from that area right away and keep at it until it's second nature or complete. Then repeat and add a second. Then a third. As we mentioned earlier, when you focus on everything, you focus on nothing. Start small with one simple thing and build on it over time.

> Small deeds done are better than great deeds planned.
>
> – Peter Marshall

> Take the first step in faith. You don't have to see the whole staircase, just take the first step.
>
> – Martin Luther King, Jr.

As you begin, connect with our community of like-minded dads on Facebook and Twitter as well as on www.DadAthlon.com. This book is static, but the communities and website will be a dynamic source of support, sowing the seeds for future projects and ideas. Share your concerns, ideas, suggestions, and pain points. Armed with these workouts and more, we will keep training and all become elite DadAthletes.

Action steps

1) Implement one strategy from this book until it is second nature. Then repeat.
2) Take the Dad Quiz to Identify and implement your highest priority area of focus.
3) Join our community on Facebook/Twitter.

APPENDIX A

DAD HACKS AND BONUSES

Here we reproduce a list of all the Dad Hacks and Bonuses from throughout the book, organized by chapter.

Chapter 1: How to Use This Book

Dad Hack: Take the Quiz. What kind of dad are you? To help you prioritize which areas you may want to begin with, visit www.DadAthlon.com/DadQuiz. You will find a simple set of questions to provide clarity and direction on where to begin. This guidance provides insight into which muscle groups will benefit most from focused attention.

Chapter 2: Connecting With Daughters

BONUS: I know what you're thinking. "Maybe *he* cried, but clearly he has issues. I'm a tough guy." I'm completely fine with both assertions. But there's only one way to know for sure. Take the Butterfly challenge yourself: www.DadAthlon.com/Daughters Let me know how you do.

Dad Hack: One great book to use for your daughters is *Let's Talk: Conversation Starters for Dads and Daughters*, by Michelle Watson Canfield, Ph.D. The author lays out many topics and questions for dads who want to connect with their daughters. Some issues are uncomfortable for dads, and navigating these waters without a map or a guide is scary. This book is an excellent resource. I've started this with both my daughters. While it was a little awkward going into the first date, that evaporated quickly as we got into some of the questions. It was silly and eye-opening for each of us, and each daughter later approached me asking when we could do the next one. Whenever a teenage girl comes up to her father and asks to repeat an event, you're doing something right. Thanks to this author for developing this book, which I highly recommend to dads of tween girls or older. Check it out at www.DadAthlon.com/Daughters

Bonus: While we are on the topic of books, an excellent one on developing a meaningful relationship with your successful and confident daughter is *Strong Fathers, Strong Daughters: 10 Secrets Every Father Should Know* by pediatrician and parenting expert Meg Meeker, M.D. This book is not one to read *with* your daughter but rather for you to get deeper insights into how she views both the world and her relationship with you. Some of my observations in this book are grounded in both my own experience and Dr. Meeker's rich and thoughtful treatment. I highly recommend it. She has many other great books as well, including *Boys Should be Boys*, which is also well worth reading.

Dad Hack: Sometimes our kids want to watch a movie or show that may be above their maturity pay-grade—especially the youngest kids in a family! Whether you're selecting a movie to watch with your kids or merely determining if Slaughter Porn 7 is, in fact, appropriate for your twelve-year-old to watch at their friend's birthday party, Common Sense Media is a great resource to gauge the appropriateness of many movies and TV shows as well as books and video games. https://www.commonsensemedia.org/.

They provide not only their own target ages but also post what ages other parents and kids think as well as summaries of the plots and themes. They also provide category scores from one to five on language, violence, sex, and positive messages, among others. This is particularly handy when navigating worthwhile R-rated movies for younger teens. Perhaps you are okay with language but want to avoid sexy scenes. For example, when you look up *The Shawshank Redemption*, it observes:

- "Gritty prison tale has positive messages, lots of profanity."
- Common Sense says 16+,
- Parents say 15+
- Kids say 14+.
- Positive Messages: 4/5
- Language: 3/5
- Sex: 2/5
- Violence: 4/5

Dad Hack: Tips for writing notes to your daughter. Use a pen, not a printer. Say something along the lines of, "I love you. I'm proud of you in ways and for things you don't even know you have. God has big plans for you, and I can't wait to see what they are. I am always here for you, no matter what. I love/admire your heart/laugh/empathy." Make it unique to your daughter. And if you happen to have more than one daughter, for the sake of all that is holy, write individualized letters to each of them—notes that could *only* be for them.

Chapter 3: Connecting With Sons

Dad Hack: Audible: Busy dads often don't have as much time to read as they'd like. Audiobooks provide an easy way to consume books while also doing something else, especially driving or running. Owned by Amazon, Audible has an enormous catalog of books. It allows you to download and listen to audiobooks cheaply and easily. Learn more about how it works at www.DadAthlon.com/audible. Want to kick it up a notch? Narrators talk slowly. Use the Audible app and listen to books at 1.25x or 1.5x or even 2x speed, which is closer to the pace of normal human speech. This also helps you get through the books in half the time. Listen during your commute or when exercising, and you can knock out a normal length book in a week or less without setting aside any additional time.

Dad Hack: Free Tennis Balls: Want a million free tennis balls to pitch to your kids? Head to your local tennis club. Once tennis balls lose their freshness, the club typically just tosses them. Head over and ask if they have any old or used tennis balls they'd like to get rid of. The first time I did that, I got a trash bag full!

Chapter 4: Connecting With Mom

Bonus: If you are really committed to this planning idea, you might even consider setting aside a full day or weekend for a couple's annual planning retreat developed by The ONE Thing. Some are in person, and others are online. These retreats provide a great way to connect with each other and connect with your goals and values as a family. Plus, you'll map out a plan to get there. Check out www.DadAthlon.com/Mom for more info as well as a link to this resource.

Chapter 5: Execution

Dad Hack: Putting money where your mouth is. Are you *really* serious about accountability? Confident you can do it? Interested in kicking it up a notch? While shame can be a powerful motivator, dollars can really make things move! Several websites motivate you to hit your goal by putting your own money on the line if you don't achieve it. Many are in the fitness and weight loss space, but not all of them. Hit your goal and get your money back, plus more. Miss your goal and lose the money you put up. You are literally putting your money where your mouth is. Here are a few worth checking out:

> www.waybetter.com: Fitness and weight-related. DietBet and StepBet live under this brand, and you bet money to hit certain weight or activity goals over two to six weeks.

> www.stickk.com: Broader than fitness only. Create any goal you want to be customized using a Commitment Contract. Non-fitness examples include "Work eight hours per week on future income stream," "Recharge or Family Time once a week," and "Write or edit one blog post per week."

> www.beeminder.com: You can set any type of goal. This app provides daily prompts to enter progress and tracks the data on detailed graphs. Go off the rails, and your credit card is charged.

Bonus: Daily Habit Self-Meeting Agenda

Date:

What is my target habit?

Is my target habit aligned with my goal?

Have I been doing it consistently? Is it baked into my bones?

If not, why?

    Not enough time? Shorten it to _____

    Wrong time of day? Move it to _____

    Distracted by something less important? Rethink your environment. Relocate it to _____

    Pushed aside by something more important? Reassess priorities. Do I need to replace this habit with a new one that is better aligned with my current priorities?

If yes…

    Am I ready to add a new goal/habit?

    Which one do I want to add?

    Is this habit alone sufficient to achieve my current goal?

    Do I need another habit that accelerates my progress toward my current goal or one that supports a different goal?

    What is the next most important thing on my list?

What is the next skill/habit I need most right now?

What is the *smallest* daily action I know I can do *every day* to support this new habit?

How can I stack this easily on top of my current habit(s)?

Chapter 6: Dollars - Defense

BONUS: Interested in seeing my slides? Take a look www.DadAthlon.com/Dollars. There are only 25 slides, and it goes pretty quick. Let me know what you think.

Dad Hack: One resource that makes viewing all your accounts and transactions easy is a financial aggregator. After setting it up with the login details from all your accounts, these sites provide a thorough picture of your *entire* financial health. This makes the process of finding leaks a one-stop shop. You can see reports like what categories you spend the most on and your net worth over time.

Some banks and financial advisors themselves offer versions of this service, so check with yours.

Or you can sign up for a free account at Mint—which will connect your accounts and help you track most expenses. www.mint.com

Personal Capital has useful free tools. It provides more robust reporting and planning for a fee if you're interested in deeper analysis or guidance. www.personalcapital.com

Each serves a slightly different purpose, and as such, each has its pros and cons depending on your needs.

Dad Hack: ReFi + Consolidate. With interest rates so low, refinancing a mortgage will reduce your monthly payment. But if you have adequate equity in your home, you may also be able to take out some extra cash to pay off other debt, like credit cards or car loans. The rate will be a little higher than if you do not take cash out, but this may be worthwhile if it still lowers your rate and you can extinguish some other debt. That lowers both your monthly expenses and the total amount of interest you would pay your creditors over time. Only one catch: *don't* run up the balance again on your credit card. Consider cutting up the cards, and don't go out and buy another car! For additional resources and information on ReFi, visit www.DadAthlon.com/Dollars

Dad Hack: Easy to use escrow account: For years, we have used Capital One 360. You can set up accounts in five minutes for free. Funding and transfers are easy and free. They are a reputable bank and pay higher than average interest rates on savings accounts, which is what we use for our escrows. You can have a ton of accounts if you decide you have many categories you want to pre-fund. The only semi-downside is that transfers to and from external accounts take two to three days. If you are using the accounts as suggested above, that isn't a problem since you wouldn't need large amounts of cash immediately. We've had accounts there since 2001, and they work very well for this purpose.

Bonus: Capital One 360 also has great accounts for kids and teens, which you can link easily to your adult accounts. This encourages your kids to save and spend wisely. It also enables oversight and easy, immediate transfers for mowing the lawn or going to the movies.

Dad Hack: Split Direct Deposit. Many people have their paycheck directly deposited into their checking account. But what they do *not* know is that most of the time, that money can be deposited into several different accounts. This is not nearly as tricky as most people think it is. Call your HR/payroll person, and likely you'll have only a very simple half-page form to complete. Within two or three pay cycles, you can have $500 go here, $250 go there, and the rest into your normal checking account.

Chapter 7: Dollars - Offense

Dad Hack: Financial Offense Goal Planner. Take ten minutes and write down what specific goals you have for your kids and family that are tied to dollar amounts. Think about how much you need and when. Compare that to how much you have and will continue to earn. Will you have enough, or is there a gap? How big is the gap? *That* is your financial offense goal you should work toward as you plan your offense.

Dad Hack: Balancing your time visualization: *Before* diving into a side hustle, take a moment to step back and imagine having a conversation with your *adult* children. Before you move forward in the present, clarify if the tradeoff is worth it to your *future* children. That is why you're doing all this, after all. So it makes sense to get their opinion. Ask *them* if they understand why you did this. Ask *them* if they think the cost was worth the tradeoff. In your mind, they are adults, so let *that* version of them come through. Were they able to go to college because you only went to one game per week instead of two? Or did they always have the newest iPhone but never saw you? Let them be honest.

Chapter 8: Health

Dad Hack: Fitness Apps: Here are a few useful apps and tools that have worked for me.

> - My Fitness Pal: An app to set goals, easily track calories—in and out—and get info and support. The free version has all these features, and premium kicks them up a notch.

- Zero Intermittent Fasting: An app to set goals and track hours between meals. Many types of fasts are available.
- Beachbody on Demand: Tons of workouts and programs of every duration, intensity, and fitness level. Coaching as well. Not free, but well worth the cost and likely a lot less than your local gym.
- Peleton: No, you don't need the bike. Like Beachbody, this membership has many types and styles of workouts you can do from anywhere with or without a bike.

Dad Hack: Options for remote therapy. Dads are all very busy, and not having time to take care of the goose isn't just something we make up. Sometimes we need to find a solution that balances the needs we have with the time we have. Needing support no longer requires us to take a half-day off work. Technology now allows us to have our cake and eat it too. Options exist that provide fully trained and licensed psychologists and therapists that fit into our busy lives. Options range from fully live sessions to text and audio support. We can get the assistance we need without leaving the house or even while we're commuting. Some good options to consider are:

- Better Help https://www.betterhelp.com/
- Talkspace https://www.talkspace.com/online-therapy/

Chapter 9: Joy

Dad Hack: The Perseid Meteor shower is an annual event. It typically peaks around August 12 every year as the earth passes through the same debris from the Swift Tuttle comet. You'll see more action before dawn than in the late evening because the earth's rotation will be the same direction as its motion through space, which means the sky passes through more meteors as it moves through the field more quickly. Now you can plan accordingly.

Dad Hack: Family-friendly comedians. You may know a few of these names already, but here is a list of very funny comedians you can watch with your kids. Some are young, others have been around a while, but funny is funny. Preview them on YouTube or a streaming service first to verify that they are *your* kind of clean and also that you think they are funny: Jim Gaffigan, Brian Regan, Jerry Seinfeld, Ellen Degeneres, Bob Newhart, Nate Bargatze, Bill Engvall, Ryan Hamilton, Michael, Jr. The Carol Burnett Show

APPENDIX B

DOS AND DON'TS

Below is a list of each chapter's Dos organized by chapter, followed by each chapter's Don'ts.

Do

Chapter 1: How to Use this Book

- Read the whole book.
- Take the assessment at www.DadAthlon.com/DadQuiz.
- Pick *one* area to focus on first.
- Reread the chapter on your primary area of focus and implement your first strategy until it's mastered.
- If you still need to build strength, pick a new strategy in the same chapter, focusing on one at a time until you feel good about your progress.

Then…

- Move on to your next highest area of focus.
- Repeat.

- Join our DadAthlon Facebook Group
- Follow us on Twitter @DadAthlon

Chapter 2: Connecting With Daughters

- Set aside purposeful time to spend with your daughter regularly. Schedule it on your calendar.
- Take advantage of tiny moments before bed or during breakfast to check in with a prayer or a word for the day.
- Create clear boundaries and enforce them firmly with love.
- Read a book with your daughter or read her favorite book and ask her about it.
- Make a list together of movies and TV shows to watch with your daughter and schedule regular time to watch them
- Learn a card game together or teach her.
- Write handwritten notes about how much you love her.
- Be an example of the person you would like her to marry.

Chapter 3: Connecting With Sons

- Be the man you want your son to grow into.
- Let him see you make mistakes, take responsibility, and fix them.
- Plan time with your son doing active events like concerts, arcades, axe-throwing, or laser tag.
- Make a list of kickass movies, old and new, to watch together.
- Get actively involved in coaching, scouts, or whatever activity he's interested in.
- Get to know his friends.
- Tell him he's awesome in writing or in person.
- Check-in and have deeper, more meaningful conversations when necessary.

Chapter 4: Connecting With Mom

- Set up a time to clarify your roles, preferably over coffee, cocktails, or dinner.
- Put special days in your calendar a week in advance.
- Fill her cup regularly with appreciation and validation.
- Actively seek ways to recharge her batteries, with *and* without you.
- Brag about her publicly, especially in front of your kids.
- Schedule regular time with her to manage the family, but make it enjoyable.
- Allow her to support *you*.

Chapter 5: Execution

- Sit down and get clear about what you want most.
- Pick the one area you want to strengthen first and create a simple plan that moves you in that direction.
- *Focus* on building that habit.
- Track your habits daily and visibly.
- Check-in with yourself regularly to assess if the habit is installed or the goal is achieved.

Chapter 6: Dollars - Defense

- Find the leaks—review twelve months of transactions to determine where your money is going.
- Fix the leaks—categorize the leaks into one of the following fixes:
    - Eliminate
    - Reduce/Renegotiate
    - Plan For/Variable with Benefits

- Create a simple budget where every type of expense is one of the following:
  - Fixed/AutoPilot
  - Variable with Benefits
  - Discretionary
- Set up escrow accounts for all Plan For/VarB items so that you can budget for them as a Fixed/Autopilot item. This leads to budget-buster immunity.
- Set up prepaid debit cards for the 2-4 expense types that fall under Discretionary. The fewer, the better.
- Modify your direct deposits so that the appropriate amounts are automatically whisked away into these pre-planned buckets.

Chapter 7: Dollars - Offense

- Get clear and specific on *why* you want to earn more—to save how much, for what, by when?
- Determine if your goals require a one-and-done solution or a steady higher cash flow.
- If one-and-done, pick a strategy and implement it. If you don't reach your goal, pick another and try that.
- If your goals require steady cash flow, determine your priorities in the Success Matrix. This ensures your plan addresses the requirements of time, knowledge, location, and enjoyment. Complete the Success Matrix Cheat Sheet to select a side-hustle that works well for you.
- Be realistic about how much time and effort you can allocate to your selected strategy.

Chapter 8: Health

- ➢ Take time to feed your goose.
- ➢ Schedule a real appointment in your calendar to do something that fills your tank.
- ➢ Implement one small habit into your morning that supports an area of need: body, mind, or heart.
- ➢ Once it's second nature, implement another.

Chapter 9: Joy

- ➢ Seek out opportunities for memories.
- ➢ Celebrate our kids with stories about them *to* them and *for* them.
- ➢ Capture memories in writing, pictures, and videos.
- ➢ Let your kids *see* you being proactive about creating joy in their lives.

Chapter 10: Wisdom

- ➢ Teach your kids about your faith.
- ➢ Talk to them about your failures and what you learned.
- ➢ Own your mistakes and take responsibility, both with them and with others in front of them.
- ➢ Capture the wisdom you've acquired in your life—for you *and* your kids.
- ➢ Finally:
    - o Do what you say.
    - o Say what you mean.
    - o Mean what you do.

Don't

Chapter 1: How to Use This Book

- ➢ Implement multiple strategies at the same time
- ➢ Get discouraged after a bad day/week/month

Chapter 2: Connecting with Daughters

- ➢ Let your busy-ness or discomfort become an excuse to delay spending time together.
- ➢ Rationalize that "she knows I love her."
- ➢ Assume she doesn't need you. Even if that is what she says.
- ➢ Behave in a way that allows your daughter to believe anything less than that she is valuable and precious beyond measure.

Chapter 3: Connecting With Sons

- ➢ Assume he's fine because he hasn't said anything is bothering him.
- ➢ Pretend you're perfect.
- ➢ Disrespect his mother.
- ➢ Let mom have all the hard conversations.

Chapter 4: Connecting With Mom

- ➢ Disrespect her at all, and especially in front of the kids.
- ➢ Have secrets with the kids from her, unless it is a surprise *for* her.

- Complain about her publicly.
- Keep your own needs secret.
- Behave like you're an extra kid.

Chapter 5: Execution

- Try to accomplish it all at once.
- Try to install two habits at once.
- Assume a habit, once installed, will stay forever without a reason.

Chapter 6: Dollars - Defense

- Wait
- Skimp on the number of months you analyze.

Chapter 7: Dollars Offense

- Put in place a strategy without thinking about it carefully first.
- Underestimate the time commitment your strategy will require.
- Do anything you hate.
- Ignore what your future kids would say about how *they'd want you to spend* your time.

Chapter 8: Health

- Overbook your schedule.
- Kill your goose.

Chapter 9: Joy

- ➢ Make jokes at your kids' expense.
- ➢ Wait to write down your memories and stories.
- ➢ Be *so* concerned about capturing the joy that you're not living the joy—or worse, ruining it for the kids!

Chapter 10: Wisdom

- ➢ Bullshit your kids.
- ➢ Shrug your shoulders on life's most important questions.
- ➢ Be passive.
- ➢ Avoid hard conversations with your kids on real issues just because you may not have a good answer.

APPENDIX C

USEFUL LINKS

Below is a list of links to the resources discussed throughout the book, organized by chapter.

www.DadAthlon.com/DadQuiz
Take the Quiz to learn your Dad Type and where you should focus your efforts first.

www.DadAthlon.com/audible
Save time reading books by listening to them while driving or exercising.

Use this link to get your first book free!

www.DadAthlon.com/FreeAudio
Download the audio version of *Dad On Purpose* absolutely FREE.

www.DadAthlon.com/Daughters
Take the Butterfly challenge and see if you cry too.

Excellent book of conversation starters and dates with your daughter

https://www.commonsensemedia.org/ Great resource for gauging age-appropriateness of movies, shows, books, and video games.

Movies Perfect movies to watch with your daughter.

Watching Touching song <u>by Mark Schultz</u> illustrating how much your kids are paying attention to you.

www.DadAthlon.com/Sons
Cool movies to watch with your son.

Great books to read with you your son.

www.DadAthlon.com/Mom
https://www.the1thing.com/resources/kick-ass-guide-to-your-couples-goal-setting-retreat/ (Re)connect with your wife using this resource to get on the same page on your biggest priorities.

https://www.5lovelanguages.com/quizzes/couples-quiz/ Connect more effectively with your wife by understanding better how you each need to experience love.

www.DadAthlon.com/Execution
Create external accountability with these websites:

  www.waybetter.com
  www.stickk.com
  www.beeminder.com

Habit Agenda: Review and track your progress and adjust as necessary with this weekly habit self-meeting agenda

The Miracle Morning book, by Hal Elrod

Atomic Habits book by James Clear

www.DadAthlon.com/Dollars

Lights: Check out my neurotic and harmlessly overbearing dad-rant on the value of shutting off the damn lights.

Get a one-stop snapshot of all your financial data using one of these aggregator sites:

> www.mint.com
> www.personalcapital.com

ReFi Resources: https://www.bankrate.com/mortgages/refinance-rates Get current refinance rates and details from several lenders and apply.

College Spreadsheet: Check out a sample spreadsheet to plan for and track college expenses.

https://www.decluttr.com/how-it-works/ Sell electronics, toys, and more around your house easily.

Use these websites to sell various types of books:

> https://bookscouter.com/
> https://www.sellbackyourbook.com/
> https://www.bookfinder.com/buyback/

www.americangemsociety.org/gems-and-jewelry/sell-your-fine-jewelry/ Sell non-sentimental jewelry using tips from this expert's site.

Offer your virtual assistant skills and services at one of these websites:

> Zirtual: https://www.zirtual.com/
> PeoplePerHour: https://www.peopleperhour.com/
> VANetworking: https://www.vanetworking.com/

Earn extra money tutoring kids remotely in an area of expertise or English as a foreign language at one of these websites:

>Tutor.com: https://www.tutor.com/
>Care.com: https://www.care.com/
>Teachaway.com: https://www.teachaway.com/blog/8-amazing-companies-let-you-teach-english-online-from-home
>https://www.teachaway.com/schools/vipkid

Earn extra dough by performing any of a wide array of "gig" services on one of these platforms:

>Fiverr: https://www.fiverr.com/
>Upwork: https://www.upwork.com/

Earn a few extra dollars doing local in-person jobs at one of these platforms:

>Craigslist: https://www.craigslist.org/about/sites
>Handy.com: https://www.handy.com/services.
>Taskrabbit: https://www.taskrabbit.com/

www.DadAthlon.com/Health

Access mental health professionals easily and conveniently on one of these sites:

>Better Help https://www.betterhelp.com/
>Talkspace https://www.talkspace.com/online-therapy/

www.DadAthlon.com/Joy

Halloween: Awesome Kick-ass Dad Halloween Hacks
Geocaching: Fun outside with pre-canned treasure hunts
Find tickets to your kids' favorite concerts at one of these sites:

>www.Bandcamp.com

www.Bandsintown.com
www.TicketMaster.com
www.LiveNation.com

www.DadAthlon.com/Wisdom
Links to books and resources that are great sources of wisdom

APPENDIX D

OTHER GREAT BOOKS

There are many excellent books on parenting, goal-setting, and success. I am especially indebted to the authors of these books not only for their role in providing valuable insights for certain aspects of this book, but also and more importantly, in helping me craft the better version of my life that my kids, my wife, and I deserve. Find links to these books and more at www.DadAthlon.com/Books.

Let's Talk: Conversation Starters For Dads and Daughters by Michelle Watson Canfield, Ph.D

Strong Fathers Strong Daughters by Meg Meeker, M.D.

Boys Should be Boys by Meg Meeker, M.D.

The 5 Love Languages by Gary Chapman

The Total Money Makeover by Dave Ramsey

7 Habits of Highly Effective People by Stephen Covey

The Miracle Morning by Hal Elrod

Atomic Habits by James Clear

Your Best Year Ever: A 5-Step Plan for Achieving Your Most Important Goals by Michael Hyatt

ACKNOWLEDGMENTS

A very special thank you to the following people, without whose support I could not have produced this book.

My editor, Amy Pattee Colvin, for her wise guidance on language, format, and grammar, all while strengthening my voice.

My audio engineer, Jamie Kent, for his helpful support and excellent technical acumen in bringing to life the audio version of this book.

My Self-Publishing School coach, Brett Hilker, for his invaluable advice and ideas on all the nitty gritty parts of the book publishing process no one knows.

The Self-Publishing School community for their supportive feedback throughout the arduous process of writing and publishing a book.

Libby Hawkins from Commit Action, for motivating me and helping to hold me accountable to myself in our weekly calls.

My wife, Erin, for her advice on the text, her friendship, and her steadfast goodness, which inspires me every day to become a better man than I was yesterday.

ABOUT THE AUTHOR

As a father of boys & girls, twins & singles, and toddlers & teenagers, *Dad On Purpose* author Tim Dunn has learned humility and tenacity from a wide variety of parenting missteps. Working as an insurance executive for over 25 years while also coaching, traveling, and dadding, he understands first-hand the importance of balance to a father and his family.

He is the founder of DadAthlon.com, a community dedicated to helping fathers achieve balanced strength across all aspects of fatherhood.

When not in the zone, Tim enjoys nerdy podcasts, classic movies, and shutting off lights around the house. He lives in central Connecticut with his wonderful wife Erin, their four kids, and their rescue dog Pepper, whom he begrudgingly loves.

THANK YOU

Pepper and I really appreciate you taking the time to read my book, and hope you found it helpful.

I'd love to get your input to ensure future editions as well as follow-up books are as valuable as possible.

Please leave me a helpful review on Amazon to let me know your thoughts.

Thanks very much.

All the best,

~Tim Dunn

Made in the USA
Middletown, DE
06 October 2023